NATIVE MEN OF COURAGE

Vincent Schilling

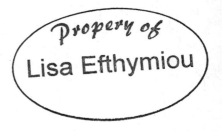

7th GENERATION

NATIVE VOICES
Summertown, Tennessee

Library of Congress Cataloging-in-Publication Data

Schilling, Vincent.
    Native men of courage / Vincent Schilling.
        p. cm. — (Native trailblazer series)
    ISBN 978-0-9779183-3-1
    1. Indians of North America—Biography—Juvenile literature.   I. Title.

E89.S13 2008
920'.009297—dc22
[B]

2008007458

Published in the United States by
7th Generation
P.O. Box 99
Summertown, TN 38483
(888) 260-8458

Printed in Canada.

ISBN 978-0-9779183-3-1

Photo credits found on page 117.

Seventh Generation is committed to preserving ancient forests and natural resources. We have elected to print this title on paper which is 100% postconsumer recycled and processed chlorine free. As a result of our paper choice, we have saved the following natural resources:

36 trees

1,685 pounds of solid waste

13,125 gallons of water

3,162 pounds pounds of greenhouse gases

25 million BTUs of total energy

For more information, visit
www.greenpressinitiative.org.

(Paper calculations from Environmental Defense Paper Calculator: www.papercalculator.org)

I dedicate this book to Mary Schilling.

You helped me to become the person that I am today.

You always believed that I would do great things.

Vincent Schilling is an enrolled member of the St. Regis Mohawk Tribe. He loves to travel and has seen nearly half of the United States by car. He considers himself to be an amateur photographer. He also enjoys many athletic activities such as bicycling, snow skiing and swimming.

This is the second book Vincent has authored. His first book *Native Athletes in Action!* highlights the lives of 13 outstanding Native athletes, both men and women. As with his last book, Vincent spoke directly to all the courageous men included in his book. He found the all the men to be both amazing and inspirational.

Vincent Schilling

He now lives in Virginia Beach with his beautiful wife Delores.

CONTENTS

CHAPTER 1

Golden Eagles Hotshots (SYCUAN RESERVATION)

NATIVE AMERICAN WILD LAND FIREFIGHTERS

CHAPTER 2

Patrick Brazeau (ALGONQUIN)

NATIONAL CHIEF OF THE CONGRESS OF ABORIGINAL PEOPLES

CHAPTER 3

Red Hawk (CHEROKEE)

SPIRITUAL LEADER, ARTIST, AND PUBLIC SPEAKER

CHAPTER 4

Larry Merculieff (ALEUT)

COMMUNITY LEADER

CHAPTER 5

Chief Frank Abraham (OJIBWE)

LITTLE BLACK RIVER FIRST NATION

So many people contribute to the process of creating a book. I would like to thank every one of them and I will do my best to do so. If I have forgotten anyone, it does not mean anything other than a human error. My gratitude for everyone's effort is genuine.

First I would like to thank everyone at Book Publishing Company. Without the help and input from Kathleen Hanson, Jerry Hutchens, Bob Holzapfel, Warren Jefferson, Gwynelle Dismukes, Anna Pope and others at BPC, gifts to the world such as *Native Men of Courage* would never materialize. Because of your efforts, many lives can change for the better.

Second, I want to thank my wife Delores Schilling. She is my greatest supporter and wise beyond her years. There can never be enough words to express my thanks. This book is as much because of you as me. I love you Delores.

I want to thank all of my family, especially my father Ray Schilling and the incredible woman who helped raise me; Mary Schilling. It is to you that I dedicate this, my second book.

I also thank my wife's family who has taken me under their wing. Thank you to Sharon Anderson, Mary Keller and my little man Parker.

And within the process, there have been those who have been supportive and lent their efforts to help make this book possible. Thank you to Henry Martin, Kathy Flores (my research helper) and Dann Boyko (you are a great friend buddy) who have provided an endless amount of moral support.

Hello also to Natalie Bruffy, Cera Beck, Chloe Beck and Ruby Christian, you will always be my friends. To Mary White, (another gifted writer) keep up your dreams Mary, everything you do is based on the spirit of selfless service, I admire you. And to Doris and Bill Anderson, you both have been very supportive.

Thank you to the staff of the Virginia Beach Library system, especially the Kempsville Library. Thank you also to Rene Ball and Margie Long of the Virginia Beach Police Department, Al Fleming of the CAP, and to Dave Devendorf and Nancy Tierney, staff members to Senator Campbell.

But thank you most of all to the courageous men in this book, including a special mention to the Golden Eagles Hotshots, especially Chief Ruiz. You guys treated me like a king, and I will always think of you as my brothers. I wish this book was a million pages long to give all of you the credit you deserve.

Also, a note of thanks to Red Hawk and Senator Campbell, I will always cherish having met with you.

All of the men in this book are honorable and heroic, I am a better person because of their combined wisdom. Their words will influence positive change and help the lives of so many. I am forever grateful to you and what you do. Thank you to all of you—You all are exactly what the title of this book indicates—You are all Native Men of Courage.

hat defines courage? I have heard many explanations of courage in my life. "Courage is fear holding on one moment longer" is one definition that has always stayed with me. I have done "courageous" things in my life and I have held my breath while I did them, but I usually didn't realize what I had done was courageous until the moment passed. I was sure about one thing though, I was scared and it took a lot of courage to finish what I needed to do.

When the opportunity came to write a book about courageous men, I became excited. Now was my chance to meet some real heroes. In the midst of my interviews for the book, I found myself in situations that one year ago I never would have thought possible. I went to Washington D.C. to meet with the retired Senator Ben Nighthorse Campbell. I was in a small café with Chief Red Hawk, a man who oversees the needs of countless Cherokee people. I accompanied Lieutenant Mark Bowman in his patrol car as he surveyed his precincts in Virginia Beach. I also found myself on the front lines of a forest wildfire in Marion County North Carolina to interview Chief Raymond Ruiz and members of the Golden Eagle Hotshots. I remember thinking to myself many times . . . "now these are definitely men of courage!"

To be in situations these courageous men find themselves in is mind blowing. Chief Red Hawk speaks before crowds of thousands of people every year, Ben Campbell has had his nose broken nine times in his quest to become a better judo competitor, and he has made decisions that affected an entire nation. The Golden Eagle Hotshots and Lieutenant Mark Bowman enter into the line of danger every time they do their job.

I talked to men who have faced darkness and arose truly triumphant. Surgeon Stanley Vollant faced incredible racism and fought his worst fears to become a leading surgical doctor in Ottawa Canada. Ojibwe Chief Frank Abraham spoke out against some of his relatives in the quest to accomplish what was right. Attorney Raymond Cross went up against the Federal Government to fight for his own people because he felt the fight was the right thing to do.

All of these men are courageous. Some fought, some resisted and some spoke out, but regardless of the physical actions of what they did, they all listened to their hearts and acted in accordance to what they knew was best. These men are all warriors.

To speak to such a group of men has been an incredible honor. And to learn from their words does not compare to any experience I have ever had. They have changed my perspectives on many things in my life, and for that, I am eternally grateful.

Golden Eagles Hotshots

NATIVE AMERICAN WILD LAND FIREFIGHTERS

I f you are in the midst of battling a ferocious wild-fire and you're pulling up a snag after the sawyer team paved the way for your other crewmembers to cut and scrape a line, chances are you are a firefighter with the Golden Eagles Hotshots.

Back Row: Miguel Garcia, Jesus Quiroz, Bryan Harward, Jeffery Citriniti, Jerry Stoltz. *Center:* Ray Ruiz Sr., Byron Alcantara, Rick Madrigal, Christopher Rivera, Michael Smolcich, Luis Guzman, Bryan Jean, Juan Mendez. *Front:* Leland Red Eagle, Michael Flores, Cody Ridley, Robert Villegas Jr., Teles Pablo III, Robert Goodwin

A "snag" is a small tree, and the "sawyer team" is in charge of cutting away large clumps of trees with chain saws. "Cutting and scraping a line" is a method of clearing away flammable material from the ground and creating a barrier that fire cannot cross. And the Golden Eagles Hotshots are a heroic team of firefighters, and a division of the Sycuan Fire Department, of the Sycuan Indian Reservation in Southern California.

The Golden Eagles Hotshots specialize in fighting wildfires. Of the twenty-two-man crew, nearly fifty percent are Native American. They are a culturally diverse group, with representatives from Karuk, Costanoan Rumsen, Pima, Shoshoni and Sioux. There are African-American, Filipino, Anglo and Latino crewmembers as well. However, independent of their ethnic background, what stands out about the Hotshots is their strong bond of teamwork and friendship.

Two committed men are responsible for the development and success of the Golden Eagles Hotshots. In 1974, Chief Hank Murphy, of the Sycuan Kumeyaay Nation, founded the Sycuan Fire Department and, more than thirty years later, he is still its Senior Fire Chief. He has also served as a council member on his tribal government throughout those same years. His paternal grandparents are from the La Huerta Kumeyaay community of Baja California and his maternal grandparents are from the Inaja and Sycuan Reservations in San Diego County.

The Golden Eagles Hotshots team is headed by Division Chief Raymond Ruiz Sr. Ruiz has just reached the age of fifty, yet looks at least ten years younger due to his joyful spirit and zest for his career. He loves his crew and it shows, and no conversation seems to pass without mention of the pride he has for his men. Ruiz grew up in Santiago de Las Vegas, Cuba and fled to the United States as a child with his grandparents. He lived throughout his adolescence in South Central Los Angeles and became involved with a gang. He got into trouble and ended up on probation and

Of the twenty-two-man crew, nearly fifty percent are Native American.

in a program that offered job training in firefighting. The authorities took note of his desire to do the right thing and he earned the respect of his superiors. He was asked to become a firefighter and eventually ended up in the Sycuan Reservation. His experiences as a young man have enabled him to serve as an effective teacher, mentor, and father figure for the crew of the Golden Eagles Hotshots.

The Golden Eagles Hotshots crew is funded by the Bureau of Indian Affairs (BIA) and the National Interagency Fire Center, but managed and operated by the Sycuan tribe. According to Chief Ruiz, this structure "gives us a little more flexibility. There is too much bureaucracy in the Federal Government. If you wanted to fire one guy and hire another tomorrow, there are rules and restrictions and red tape. In order for us to make our program as successful as it is, we chose to go with the tribe."

Teamwork is extremely important when fighting fires.

The tribe's training methods and rules are strict, and the leaders work hard to instill a sense of pride in all of their members. The Golden Eagles Hotshots stand out from other crews in the way they present themselves, including a strict adherence to manners and a uniform dress code. Initially, however, the pride of the Golden Eagles Hotshots was not entirely well received. According to Chief Ruiz, "There was a lot of intimidation from others. Here were these Native American crews standing at attention, and others would say, 'all they need is weapons.' They were missing the picture. We were trying to make a point, to show that we are not a bunch of stupid, drunk, and uneducated Indians. What you see is what you get, including our uniform and how we dress. We all dress the same and no one looks like an individual. When we travel, we travel with our Fire Department uniform with badges and ribbons and the whole works. Other guys might think, 'whoa, who are these guys?' But we're not trying to impress them. We are sending a message that we know what we're doing."

The Golden Eagles Hotshots work in harsh and hot conditions breathing smoke and getting burned by floating embers. They not only wear fire-resistant brush jackets and Kevlar pants; they also wear goggles, gloves, helmets and 50-pound (23-kg) gear packs that contain food, water, and safety equipment. They also carry an assortment of tools to help in the fight against fire. And don't forget: They do all of this in the hottest months of the year. Wilderness firefighting is not a job for the faint of heart!

The mission statement of the Golden Eagles Hotshots clearly expresses the commitment of the crew. Their primary mission is "to provide a safe, mobile and highly skilled crew for all aspects of wild land fire suppression and disaster mitigation" with a "highly professional, error-resilient crew." In the vision statement that follows, they confirm their goal of "strengthening the wild land fire community and Native American Nations by merging quality people of various backgrounds and ethnic groups" and respecting traditions by "preserving the past while building the future."

In June of 2007, a twenty-member crew of the Golden Eagles Hotshots was called to serve in the wilderness outside Marion City, North Carolina. They were asked to fight the Linville Gorge wildfire along with other firefighting crews from around the country and the North Carolina Division of Forestry Resources. As the Golden Eagles Hotshots headed out to fight the fire in the wilderness of Linville Gorge their presence was unmistakable. Although all of the firefighting crews had been fighting long and hard for days on end, the Golden Eagles Hotshots alone looked crisp and neat in their blue slacks and tan polo shirts. Many of the veteran crewmembers of the Golden Eagles Hotshots had shaved their heads into Mohawk haircuts—their traditional sign of support for rookies who, in Sycuan tradition, sport

Mohawks until after they fight their first fire. Rookies and veterans alike were prepared to work hard until the fires were under control.

Here are some of the courageous and committed Native fire-fighters of the Golden Eagles Hotshots who battled in North Carolina:

ROBERT GOODWIN
Karuk Tribe, Northern California

When Robert Goodwin turned eighteen, he began working with a Karuk fire crew for a summer job. His tribe then sent him to the Fire Academy at the Sycuan Reservation. After he graduated he spent his first year with the Sycuan Fire Department and was attached to the flight crew in San Diego, which meant that he got to fly in a helicopter! Robert remembers, "When the fire first starts, they drop us off and we go knock it down real quick. Then we get back on the helicopter and fly out. Once the trucks and crews get there, they contain it with their water and hoses."

One of the first things a firefighter in the wilderness learns is how to create a fire-break—a path in which the fire cannot burn any further. They "drag a line"—remove all of the flammable grass, pine needles, and leaves to expose a dirt path that will not burn. This is not an easy task in the wilderness, as there are tree roots to

As a team leader, members of his crew look up to Robert Goodwin.

dig through and sometimes even small trees that need to be cut down. A well-cut line or path can stop serious damage from a fire. Robert says, "We use hand tools, chainsaws, pulaskis, it's like an axe with a pick on the back, and McLeods, a rake with a straight blade on the end. We remove the fuel—the flammable debris—and we create a big, bare dirt trail around it. It works pretty well. If the stuff is too tall, the flame links are going to go over so you have to employ different tactics. We'll make a fire break like we do normally, but then we'll set fire so it goes toward the main fire."

Who would have expected a firefighter to set fires in order to stop fires? But every action Robert takes is done with safety in mind. "It's a risky job, but we don't go out of our way to put ourselves into real harm. We're trained and experienced enough to know a risky situation. We can turn down an assignment or find a better way of going about things rather than just jumping into a big fire. We're trained to push ourselves to the very limit. We've had guys who have had to be flown out by helicopter because of heat exhaustion and pushing themselves too hard. There are some days when I think, 'man, I'm not going to be able to keep going.' There are days when you feel like that, but at the end of the day you made it and it's a sense of accomplishment. You take a lot of pride in it and you know how far you can push yourself again."

When Robert was still a new member of the Sycuan team, he was not given the difficult and action-oriented assignments that more experienced members take on. But when the opportunity finally came, Robert was ready. "We weren't that well-established a crew, we didn't get good assignments. But then we finally got one and I was so tired! Breathing in all that smoke, my eyes were all watery. I was gagging and trying to work hard and it was a steep hill. It was such a kick in the pants that it prepared me for everything else."

Three years later, Robert has definitely paid his dues and gained a lot of valuable experience. He is a team leader and is looked up to by the other members of his crew. And as a Karuk, he knows that he brings pride to his tribe. "Coming from my town, there is a lot of negative Native American influence. I didn't grow up there from childhood and so I didn't really get into the culture. But when I came down here I met some of the other Natives and some of them had grown up on the reservations and knew a lot about their culture. This inspired me to learn about my culture. So I went back and started to talk to some of my family members and tried to get more out of it. But in that town there are a lot of negative Native Americans. I would see the guys in the trailer parks drinking out of paper bags and I thought that's what being Native was. But when I got older I got more in touch with the culture. There is a lot more purity to it. Even for the people who aren't going out and doing things like being athletes or heroes. They're still good people, and they do good things for themselves and their culture."

MICHAEL FLORES
Costanoan Rumsen Carmel Tribe, California

Michael Flores is affectionately called a rookie by his fellow crewmembers—he is a new member of the Golden Eagles Hotshots. Michael is from the Los Angeles and Pasadena area of California. He is a proud member of the Costanoan Rumsen tribe, from along the San Francisco Bay Area coastline. Due to the strong influence of his Costanoan mother, Michael actively participates in matters of his tribe and his family. He says, "They are all dancing, singing, and attending pow-wows every other Saturday. I would be dancing if I wasn't here [with the Golden Eagles Hotshots]. I've been here a month and a half."

Previously, Michael had been a Fire Explorer for the Los Angeles County Fire Department. He accompanied firefighters on ride-alongs on the fire engines. Michael graduated from high school at the age of sixteen and began taking college courses right away. By the time he was eighteen years old, his desire to fight fires got the best of him, and it wasn't long until Michael had successfully completed the Sycuan Fire Academy.

Within a short time, Michael has found himself in the midst of a five-thousand-acre wildfire in North Carolina. His first days were filled with activity. The Golden Eagles Hotshots crew was setting smaller controlled fires to prevent the spread of larger uncontrolled fires. "It was pretty exciting laying down fire. We had to move quickly. The guys on my right and the guys on my left were laying fire down too. It could come down and it could trap us. But that's why they train us—it's the excitement, it's a rush."

By the age of 18 Michael Flores knew he would be a fire fighter.

Michael has the true spirit of a firefighter. But he is also another kind of fighter, a boxer to be exact. He began boxing at the age of fifteen and is now fighting in the heavyweight division. "I'm a small guy for a heavyweight, but I knocked out a guy who was 6'5". I'm a firefighter from May to October and I'm boxing the other six months."

Michael offers encouragement to anyone wanting to be a firefighter. He enthuses, "Go for it! If you are into saving people and saving the environment, by all means go for it." He also talks passionately about what it's like to be Native American. "I've always loved being Native American; it makes me treasure things more. The animals or the earth— I don't take things for granted."

Michael Flores may be a new member of the Golden Eagles Hotshots, but his commitment and passion is real. Whether a firefighter has been on the job thirty days or thirty years, they all put their lives on the line. And they all share something in common with Michael Flores. They all have a true measure of genuine courage.

CODY RIDLEY
Shoshoni Fallon Reservation, Nevada

Cody Ridley wastes no time in admitting he made poor choices earlier in his life. His father was an alcoholic and Cody also got involved with drugs and alcohol. He was arrested and did time in the penitentiary for assault. However, Cody decided to dramatically turn his life around for the better; otherwise, he might not be around today to share his experiences with others and to make a meaningful contribution through his work with the Hotshots.

Cody Ridley servers as an example for all those who want to change their lives for the better.

After his prison term, Cody decided that he needed to change his life. He knew that he needed to learn from his own mistakes and the mistakes of others. One of the most positive changes in Cody's life came about through his decision to become a firefighter. "I started firefighting and I found out about the Hotshot crew at the Sycuan Fire Department. I started doing positive things. When I was in jail, I used to talk to groups of kids and ask, 'who here likes stealing cars?' They'd be like, 'Oh, I do, I do!' I'd say, 'You know, they've got a job like that; it's called a repossession man.' I would give them alternatives that would be more positive. There's a thin line between good and bad." Cody did turn his life around, and he has continued to make positive choices for more than ten years. He has definitely crossed over that thin line into good, and now that he is back out in the world, Cody has become a valuable and contributing member to society. As a firefighter, he continues to follow the right path.

On the front lines of a fire, Cody's job is a sawyer—he uses a chainsaw to clear the path for his other crewmembers. He remembers one particular incident with the Golden Eagles Hotshots on the flight crew: "We go into this fire that the engines couldn't access. It was really swampy and muggy. These homeless people lit this fire and there were a whole bunch of booby traps everywhere. We were real cautious going in. It was a trip, I'd never seen anything like that before."

Cody is helicopter-crew certified and continues his training with the Sycuan Fire Department. "A lot of us here are certified Firefighter 1's and EMT's (Emergency Medical Technicians). You never stop learning here. They pay for the training, and in return, we work hard for them."

Cody has become such a success through his work with the Golden Eagles Hotshots that he is often met with disbelief from people who knew him when he was younger. He says, "When people see me now, they are like, 'No way, that ain't Cody.'" He is aware of the important decisions he made and how they improved his life. He recalls, "I separated myself. The number one thing is that you have got to get out. Most people don't want to do it. You've got to get out of what your surroundings were before."

Cody does not associate with the people he once did, and stays away from negative influences. Instead, he has formed a Native Fight Club in Palm Springs, California where Native kids train for free in martial arts. Through Cody's efforts, kids who might have got into trouble and turned out bad are using their time constructively. Cody is a true hero and his story can serve as an example for all those who want to change their lives for the better.

TELES PABLO III
Pima Tribe, Arizona

Teles Pablo III was born in Sacaton, Arizona. He is part of the Gila River Indian Community, a small reservation 32 miles (50 km) south of Phoenix. Teles began his firefighting career as a camp crewmember with the Pima Agency of Fire Management, assisting firefighters at base camp with supplies. He was surprised when people at the Agency encouraged him to pursue firefighting. "I didn't really want to be a firefighter; I didn't know what I was getting into. I started out in camp crew. [But] people were seeing things in me that I didn't see in myself. [People] would say, 'You should try out for this. You should excel at that because you're good at what you're doing. You're young; you've still got a lot of years on you.' This will be my fifth year fighting fires, and oh, I love it! It takes a while to get where you're going but you've just got to keep at it."

And luckily for everyone, Teles has kept at it. Teles' ability to tell an exciting story is part of why he is so well liked by his crew. One of his most memorable firefighting moments involved the rescue of one of his own department fire trucks. A brush fire had started near an overpass of the Interstate 10 highway in California. In the excitement to contain the fire, Teles and his new Engine Boss managed to get the truck stuck in the path of the oncoming fire. He remembers the day very well. "The wind was channeling through the freeway pillars and the wind hit the fire. It spun a circle and came straight for the engine. The Fire Management Officer that was assisting us yelled, 'Protect that engine!' I got to the engine and the Engine Boss started to pump the water and gave me the hose. He shouted at me, 'Get in there, Pablo! Get in there!' I started running as fast as I could. My heart was pumping. My eyes were open wide. I saw my whole career flash before my eyes if that engine caught fire. So I got in front of the flames, and they were moving fast. I felt someone behind me; it was John Lee (the Engine Boss). I thought, 'I'm not going to die alone!' But it was so cool. I hit the base of the flames [with the water] and I'm not lying—[the fire] split into two fingers around the engine, totally around the engine! John Lee was like, 'Good job, good job.'"

Teles Pablo is dedicated to his crewmembers, family and to the young people who look up to him.

Another thing of great importance to Teles is his family. And he is happy that his career as a firefighter makes a strong impression on the people who are close to him. He says, "I've got a lot of younger family out there. That's what I try to concentrate on. I've got to get them to see what I can do. They say, 'Man, look—he's doing this and he's doing that. Maybe I want to do that too.' It's fun for them when I come home. And once in a while it's good to hear from the elder people, 'Hey, I'm proud of you.' When the kids smile and they run around me, it makes a huge difference. It makes me push myself. When they see how high they can go, and I'm hoping that they will achieve more than what I have—that's what motivates me."

Like a true hero, Teles is dedicated to his crewmembers and to his family, and to the success of the young people who look up to him.

LELAND KYLE RED EAGLE
Assiniboine/Lakota Sioux, California

Firefighting and heroism are in Leland Kyle Red Eagle's blood. His father, an Assiniboine from Saskatchewan, moved to San Diego at a young age and later became a firefighter for the Orange County Fire Department. Chief Hank Murphy, the founder of the Sycuan Fire Department, is Leland's uncle.

Leland's mother is an Oglala Lakota from the Pine Ridge Reservation in South Dakota. At an early age, she left the reservation to attend art school in San Diego where she met Leland's father. After they were married and had started a family, they moved to Riverside, California. Leland moved to San Diego two years ago.

Leland has always had a strong Native American influence in his life, which he cherishes. "I'm pretty deeply rooted in my ways. My family always traveled back to San Diego when I was younger to visit family for ceremonies, sun dances and sweat lodges. I'm pretty thick in my heritage. I know where I come from and I know where I belong. My uncle and my aunt have been trying to get me into firefighting for a long time. Last year I finally decided to go through the academy. I went through it and graduated. I was on a brush engine last year and this year I got a chance to be on the Hotshots."

Leland Kyle Red Eagle's calm manner is a source of strength to his fellow crewmembers.

Leland is a valued member of the Hotshots. His calm manner is a source of strength to the other crewmembers, and they know that Leland is a man they can trust. He speaks with great pride about the work of the Golden Eagles Hotshots. "Yesterday, when we were doing direct attack, we were coming up the slope and they sent six of us up there to cut off the fire from coming up the ridge. They sent out Ridley and Pablo, the Saw team, first, to cut down any hanging coverage. Stoltz and Mikey and myself followed in behind them scratching a line. We were pretty much right up in the flames. It was really hot in there!" Ultimately, Leland and his crewmembers were successful in containing the blaze.

To those interested in becoming this kind of hero, Leland has this to say: "It's going to take a lot of hard work! You have to be cautious and think clearly. You've got to know what you're doing, stay calm in tough situations and never lose your cool. You've got to love it! You can't be out here if you don't love this job."

These are some of the brave Golden Eagles who fought to contain the fire in North Carolina. The residents of Marion City were relieved that a potential disaster had been prevented by the courage, professionalism, and brave actions of these firefighters.

Dennis Wahler, a Forest Ranger with the North Carolina Division of Forestry Resources, put it this way: "All things considered, the ground forces, the resources they used—they just did an outstanding job. They ought to be commended for what they did."

But perhaps the most important praise of all comes from the words of Chief Raymond Ruiz, who speaks from the heart when he says, "I've got a great group of young men. Some have been misled, some have taken the wrong track. But God derailed them and got them back on the right track. They've been given hope, and they've given the Sycuan Fire Department an opportunity to teach them a new career and a new trade. We are given compliments

There are close to one hundred Interagency Hotshot Crews (IHC)—elite teams of professional wild land firefighters—across North America. These crews of multi-skilled professional firefighters uphold a tradition of excellence. Their physical fitness standards, training requirements, and operation procedures are consistent nationwide, and ensure that their core values of "duty, integrity, and respect" are maintained. The Hotshot crews, whose motto is "Safety, Teamwork, Professionalism"—have an excellent reputation throughout the United States and Canada.

Other Native Hotshot crews include the Rio Bravo Hotshots, the Geronimo Hotshots, the Bear Paw Hotshots, and the Mescalero Hotshots. As well, you can depend on the Color Country III Navajo Firefighters or the BIA Department of Forestry Cherokee Firefighting crew, among many others, for their heroic efforts in saving the environment and its inhabitants from the ravages of fire.

everywhere we go. We're not drunk, we're not stupid. We contribute to society and to the Fire Services. We know what we're doing."

The men under the guidance of Division Chief Raymond Ruiz were able to leave North Carolina with their heads held high. Their work was hot and demanding, dangerous and challenging, yet they didn't quit until the job was done. Professionals whose heroic actions are worthy of tremendous praise, the Golden Eagles Hotshots will long be remembered in Marion City.

Patrick Brazeau

NATIONAL CHIEF OF THE CONGRESS OF ABORIGINAL PEOPLES

At first glance, Patrick Brazeau looks too young to hold the important position of National Chief. Many others thought the same thing on November 3, 2006, when Patrick, at just 32 years of age, was named National Chief of the Congress of Aboriginal Peoples (CAP) in Canada. Many people associate youth with inexperience, but when you review the list of Patrick's achievements, it's clear that he is more than capable of leading such an important organization.

Although today Patrick proudly claims his heritage as Algonquin, his Native identity was problematic for him in his youth. Patrick was born in Maniwaki, Quebec, close to the Kitigan Zibi Anishinabeg Reserve, which is one of nine Algonquin communities situated along the Ottawa River. Patrick's grandmother was born on the reserve, but she was forced to move away after she married a non-Native man. In Canada before 1985, Native

Patrick Brazeau

women who married non-Natives lost their government status and had to leave the reserve. They were no longer legally considered "Indian." This practice changed in 1985 when the Federal Government passed an amendment to the Indian Act that gave Indian status back to Native women and their families. For Patrick, this legal change meant that suddenly, at the age of eleven, he was recognized as an Algonquin, as a status Indian for the first time.

Since Patrick grew up very close to the Kitigan Zibi reserve, he had many friends and relatives who lived on the reserve. Even so, Patrick was often scorned for not being Native enough. "Where I grew up is not indicative of my lifestyle or 'Indian-ness.' For some people, [living on a reserve] is a prerequisite. If you haven't lived on a reserve, you're not a real Indian. I certainly don't believe it. Unfortunately, it's been instilled in a lot of people. To my non-Aboriginal friends, I was too much Indian for them. To the people living on the reserve, I was not enough Indian. My dad was Indian; my mom was Métis. She was not considered Native by many people. That's why I wasn't Native enough in the eyes of some people."

Those experiences strengthened Patrick's belief that being an Indian has nothing to do with living within a federally approved reserve. These borders did not exist prior to the arrival of non-Aboriginal people and Patrick does not think they should continue to be used to define Aboriginal status. This philosophy eventually led Patrick into his current role with CAP.

Patrick was a naturally gifted student in school and maintained straight A's without having to study very hard. He was also a strong athlete and he began taking karate lessons at the age of eleven. Karate helped create the structure in his life that many of his friends and family did not have. "I was attracted to the sport because of the discipline. I grew up with some relatives who had a harder time than me. It really did teach me self-confidence and to look at situations in a different way than fighting or kicking and screaming. A lot of my relatives did not know how to respond to situations, and rightfully so, given that they were very young. I didn't have it that hard at all. I had none of those problems. But at least [karate] taught me to control some emotions." By the time he finished high school, Patrick had achieved the rank of second-degree black belt.

When he moved away from his family to make the transition to post-secondary school, Patrick had a rude awakening. "When I began my post-secondary schooling, I got into some problems with respect to grades. Up to high school, I never had to study for exams. When I started college, it was the complete opposite. I had not learned studying techniques. But I worked through it." Patrick learned how to study and his grades began to improve.

Patrick loved history and so he chose Social Sciences as his major. He eventually earned a Bachelor's degree. This was a proud moment for both Patrick and his family. After graduation, Patrick considered a future in law. He applied to a civil law program at the University of Ottawa and also to the Royal Canadian Mounted Police (RCMP) with the hopes of becoming a law enforcement officer. Ironically, Patrick received his acceptance into law school on the same day that he was accepted into the RCMP. Patrick was faced with a decision.

Patrick had heard nearly every day of his life about the frustrations felt by non-Aboriginal people toward Aboriginals. Non-Aboriginal people often assumed that Patrick and other Aboriginals didn't pay taxes and that they didn't want to work because they received financial breaks from the Federal Government. Many people wrongly assumed that Patrick was free to be lazy his entire life, never having to worry because the government paid his way. "A lot of people to this day believe those myths. But the fact remains that when an Indian person lives outside of the reserve, they pay taxes just like anybody else. There seems to be a growing frustration in the eyes of the non-Aboriginal population and taxpayers about tax dollars going toward funding of Native communities across this country. Unfortunately, there are still some communities living in third-world conditions in this great country. It's a broken system, in my opinion. That's why we need to fix it. That's why there is a lot of frustration coming from the non-Aboriginal population because if they're investing their tax dollars into this system and no positive results are being made, then it's a question of greater accountability."

With these strong political convictions, Patrick didn't have to think long about his decision. He would attend law school. He had always wanted to make a significant contribution to the cause of Aboriginal people, and the law program at the University of Ottawa would give him that chance.

Patrick did well in the program and after his second year, his involvement in the study of law led him to an exciting opportunity. Patrick was looking for work and so had sent his resumes to two national organizations in Canada. One of these, the Congress of Aboriginal Peoples, phoned Patrick and hired him for a summer position. And according to Patrick, "I have not looked back since."

At twenty-six, Patrick began working as a legal researcher for CAP. CAP's mandate is to represent Aboriginal people who do not live on reserves, as well as Canada's Métis people. Patrick's interest in Aboriginal law grew, and when the Canadian government began an initiative to increase accountability and governance on Aboriginal reserves, Patrick was hooked. He extended his stay at CAP after the summer in the

Brazeau's young age, rather than a hindrance, has helped him move forward with enthusiasm and energy.

interest of fighting for his beliefs. "Mismanagement [on reserves] was a big reason why this initiative was undertaken by the Federal Government. Right now, under the Indian Act, Chiefs and councils can basically do what they want with the funding they receive with very little accountability or reporting back to the citizens they represent. This is why the government thought it was time to increase accountability. I absolutely agreed with it. We were the only [Aboriginal] organization that supported the initiative."

CAP was stifled in its efforts to assist with the initiative. The other major Aboriginal organizations boycotted the measure because they felt that they had not been consulted. "We saw it a little differently," says Patrick. "We want to know how much money is going out to those communities, where it's being spent and more importantly, if the people who actually have needs in those communities are having access to some of those dollars. So they can get their lives back on track. Or just offer them some basic opportunities to an education and decent employment and a roof over their heads. [The goal is] just to provide those opportunities so people can later practice their own responsibility in maintaining that sort of lifestyle. My mantra is: Nobody owes anybody anything, people owe themselves."

Patrick was doing well as a legal researcher, but he found himself wanting to take a more active role with CAP. His convictions were too strong to allow him to sit idle. "Being an Aboriginal person, you sort of grow up in politics. Whether it's local politics or reserve politics, it has always been an interest of mine. I grew up admiring a lot of former Canadian prime ministers. The best way for me to get involved at that time was to get involved in Native politics."

Patrick wasted no time and sought positions with CAP where he felt he could be of most service to his people. In May 2002, Patrick was given the honor of speaking on behalf of CAP at the United Nations Permanent Forum on Indigenous Issues. He was able to highlight some of CAP's interests and concerns in a highly visible arena. In 2004, Patrick Brazeau was elected as Vice Chief of CAP. He served admirably and when the residing National Chief decided to retire in 2006, Patrick took over as interim Acting Chief. In November 2006, when the new elections were held, Patrick Brazeau became the new National Chief of The Congress of Aboriginal Peoples.

Since becoming National Chief, Patrick Brazeau has met with leaders in the Canadian government to promote and bring about positive changes for Aboriginal people. These leaders have included Cabinet members such as the Indian Affairs Minister and the Finance Minister, as well as the Governor General of Canada. Patrick's meeting with Canada's current Prime Minister, Steven Harper, has been the highlight of his career so far. Meeting with Canada's top leader gave Chief Brazeau insight into the character of the man. "It was interesting when we got a chance to meet because he wasn't as right wing as some of the comments suggested that came from other national leaders or Aboriginal leaders. We found him to be quite a balanced person and ready, willing, and able

Patrick's meeting with Prime Minister Steven Harper is a highlight of his career.

to work with anybody who was willing to work with him. That's [the policy] we adopted as an organization—we'll work with anybody who wants some positive change."

CAP focuses on establishing partnerships with the Federal Government to deal with social and economic policy issues such as job development, health, and key issues that affect fundamental individual and community rights. As leader of CAP, Patrick is committed to working with the federal, provincial and territorial governments, as well as with other national Aboriginal leaders, to ensure that the needs of off-reserve Aboriginal peoples are recognized by governments at all levels. And even though he believes in working within existing government systems, Patrick is ready to challenge them when necessary. For example, he feels strongly that The Indian Act should be abolished. The Indian Act is the set of legislations that is used to define Aboriginal status in Canada. Patrick believes the Act needs to be replaced with more progressive legislation.

The constituency of CAP comprises approximately 800,000 Aboriginal and Métis people, and, according to Patrick, "many of our members have been arbitrarily excluded from our cultural communities, lands, and access to programs and services aimed at Aboriginal People." Arbitrary definitions of "Aboriginal People" and restricted access to resources are some of the issues that Patrick sees as a priority for CAP, and his mission is to use his position to speak for the excluded and marginalized urban and rural population of Aboriginal people. And while CAP has a history of conflict with some of the other national Aboriginal organizations in Canada, Patrick's goal is to work on behalf of all Aboriginal people, and to avoid the internal battles that might slow down their progress.

Chief Brazeau's other priority is to work on behalf of Aboriginal youth. He believes strongly in the potential of youth for success through determination, hard work, and taking personal responsibility for their own future. CAP has a National Youth Council, and Patrick ensures that the members have an active voice in CAP decisions by having them hold a voting seat on the Board of Directors. Patrick encourages young people to get involved in political issues, and in a speech to Aboriginal youth, he said, "We believe that to ensure the best possible future for our peoples that you must lead the way. In addition to incorporating your needs into all aspects of policy initiatives, including those related to education, economic development, human rights, health, and the environment, we also engage in activities that have a specific youth focus." Patrick was key to the development of CAP's Annual Youth Awards that honor efforts and achievements of Aboriginal youth in the areas of Arts and Dance, Community, Culture and Heritage, Education, Leadership, and Sports. As well, CAP has been actively involved in a National Aboriginal Youth Suicide Prevention Strategy, an initiative aimed at reducing the risk and incidences of suicide among Aboriginal youth.

Patrick Brazeau's term as National Chief of the Congress of Aboriginal Peoples ends in the fall of 2008. He will have to decide whether to run for another term. Patrick definitely sees himself contributing much more to the Aboriginal cause. He also hasn't ruled out the possibility of one day running in mainstream politics. "I don't close any doors on anything. Anything is possible."

Patrick gives advice to those who may run for Chief of CAP in the future. "First and foremost, they would have to be very patient. Unfortunately, the Aboriginal agenda does not move quickly. It takes a lot of time to educate and to convince people that your method, your initiative, and your way of doing things would be better. But at the same time, it's very rewarding when you do change the life of even one person. It's going to be a constant work-in-progress. If you want your dreams fulfilled, you have to be ready to work for them. That's what I have adopted as a slogan: 'Fulfilling your dreams is all about being willing to work for them.' Because

Patrick is a family man with three children. His wife's name is Sunshine and he is happy to say he wakes up to Sunshine every morning.

that has worked for me and I think that we have to remain true to ourselves. Once you get in this business, you have to remain true to yourself or else the power and the limelight might get to you. You have to remain focused on the task at hand. This job is all about people. The commitment is to benefit people, and not get involved in political games."

Chief Patrick Brazeau has brought CAP into the national spotlight. As an advocate for change his focus has been on changing other Canadians' views of Aboriginal people. His young age, rather than a hindrance, has helped him move forward with enthusiasm and energy. "We have been in the news quite a bit because I am young and ambitious. I'm seen very often as being radical and a lot of leaders use my age as an excuse for their inaction. But I don't care what other people think of me as long as I can wake up every morning and look in the mirror and be proud of who I see. Then I'm proud and I'm satisfied with that."

The Congress of Aboriginal Peoples was founded in 1971. It was originally called the Native Council of Canada. There have been twelve presidents in its thirty-six year history, and both men and women have held the honored post, including Tony Belcourt, Viola Robinson, Dan Smith, Dwight Dorey, and Gloria George. The Board of Directors consists of representatives from all of CAP's affiliate groups, representing all provinces and territories in Canada.

Chief Patrick Brazeau is a man of courage. His successes speak highly of his people and his achievements are worthy of notice.

Today Patrick Brazeau lives in Gatineau, Quebec. He has three children: a son named Jared, and two daughters, Kegona (Algonquin for "Hope") and Patience. His wife's name is Sunshine, and Patrick is proud to say that he wakes up to Sunshine every morning.

The Indian Act of 1876 is a Canadian statute that concerns registered Indians, their bands, and the system of Indian reserves. The act allowed the Canadian government almost complete control over how Native people lived and interacted with non-Natives. At the same time, it gave the government special responsibility for the health, education, and lands of much of the Native population. The Indian Act also defines who is an "Indian" and includes legal disabilities and rights for registered Indians. Bill C-31 is the name of the 1985 Act to Amend the Indian Act. This amendment eliminated some discriminatory sections, including the one that resulted in Indian women losing their status when they married non-status men. Many people believe that the government's control of the Native population worked against the Act's stated goals, and that the Act isolated Native people from mainstream Canadian society instead of helping to integrate them into it.

Chief Red Hawk

SPIRITUAL LEADER, ARTIST, AND PUBLIC SPEAKER

I f the eyes are truly the windows to the soul, then the soul of Chief Red Hawk is as bright as the sun. At first glance, Red Hawk does not fit the stereotype of the serious, elderly Indian Chief. His youthful appearance is enhanced by his good cheer and obvious wisdom, and those fortunate enough to meet with him are guaranteed a warm hello, a gracious smile and those bright eyes.

Chief Red Hawk

Red Hawk is a full-blood Cherokee, and the Chief and President of the United Cherokee Nation. He is also a master storyteller, an award-winning musician, a very fine artist, a poet and a published author. He is a public speaker who has shared the podium with such notable people as former Secretary of Defense Colin Powell; France's Ambassador to the United States, Jean-David Levitte; actor George Okada (who played Sulu on *Star Trek*) and popular television star Judge Joe Brown.

Chief Red Hawk's home is in Virginia, but his travels have taken him to such exotic places as the Philippines, Tonga, Fuji, Samoa, Japan, and England, where he has spoken in front of more than one million people. He has written the book *Tao of an Indian,* which blends his Native wisdom with principles from Taoism, Confucianism, Buddhism, and Christianity. His resume is jam-packed with impressive accomplishments including two Telly Awards for music and nominations for "Best Spoken Word" album at the Native American Music Awards. He was awarded "diplomat" status at the 2002 Olympic Games in Salt Lake City for his performances. And he is the founder of the successful company OPM Management Solutions.

Red Hawk was born in September 1961. His father was a skilled stonemason, and although he was paid well for his work, the family often had to travel to different job site locations. When Red Hawk's mother was pregnant with him, his father was helping to build the east wing of Kansas University in Lawrence, Kansas. So Red Hawk was born there, instead of on the Cherokee reservation like his older brother. According to tribal rules, since he was born off of the reservation he was not entitled to any tribal rights. This became an important factor in his life.

When asked about his upbringing, Red Hawk doesn't hesitate to talk about the challenges he faced. He says, "There are two versions—one you tell people when you want to uplift them, and then there's the real version. Real versions are not always nice. My father was an alcoholic who went off to war, and my mother wouldn't allow us to speak our language. My father left the Reservation when he was young. He swore he would never go back because of the poverty."

Red Hawk had a strained and complicated relationship with his mother and father. Although his father provided him with an understanding of his Cherokee culture through storytelling, he was also a source of pain and confusion. "My father always called me 'little hawk' when I was growing up. In a sense I knew him completely, but I didn't know him at all. One moment he was teaching me the mysteries of the universe and another moment he was drunk, yelling and screaming. My mother wasn't that available either; she was in and out of the house. Uncles, aunts, neighbors and friends took care of us most of the time."

But Red Hawk would not let a difficult childhood get the best of him. He made positive choices for his life even though he had experienced so many incorrect choices with his family. "The beauty of being human is that you can learn, unlearn and learn it all over again if you need to. You don't have to be stuck in the way you were raised. You can say, 'I don't want to do this.' And how do you stop doing something you don't want to do? You stop it. It's easy. People say it's hard to stop. No, it isn't — you stop it."

Red Hawk grew up very close to his two brothers, Black Hawk and Swamp Rat. "Black Hawk and I were named through ceremony; Swamp Rat's name was given to him because our Grandfather had a vision. [My father] knew that Black Hawk was going to be the warrior of the family; he always sees the fight first. My life has always been a spiritual path. And Swamp Rat—you never know where he is going."

Red Hawk's spiritual path led him to teaching and guiding, and it started as early as elementary school. He often found himself on the playground, surrounded by students who eagerly listened to the stories he had learned from his father and grandfather. "My father was always a good storyteller and so was my grandfather. They would tell me stories and I would find myself echoing these stories on the playground. [For example,] how the raccoon got his black eyes—it was a fire story, and the smoke burned the raccoon's eyes. I was always the ham at the cultural shows."

Red Hawk and his brothers lived true to their namesakes. Red Hawk stayed on a path of spirituality and artistry, always lending stories to those who would listen. Black Hawk became a world champion kick boxer. "He was always taking [martial arts] lessons. He's been taking lessons since he was six or seven years old. Swamp Rat was always unpredictable. Sometimes he would just disappear. He spent time on the Lakota Reservation when the big battle of Wounded Knee took place. You could write a book just on the crazy stuff we had to bail him out of."

When Red Hawk was in high school, his father developed lung cancer and passed away. Red Hawk had already developed a spiritual understanding of death. He remembers, "It was okay. I had already been secure with life and death. We knew that for every transition there is another transition." Red Hawk moved to Arizona with his family.

As a result of his childhood experiences, Red Hawk developed a valuable understanding of family relationships. He says, "The hard part about [my] growing up is that I have half-brothers and half-sisters that I haven't talked to in thirty years. My mother, my aunts—it's the same way. In life, you have to cut out any negative energy that comes your way. I learned this from Black Hawk. If any negativity walked into that corner when he was getting ready to fight, BOOM! He was out of the corner. Everything has to be positive—no negative energy, even if that means your family members. I think it's a misunderstanding [of] the scriptures, the talk about honoring the father and mother. I think it's talking about the spiritual father. And the opposite of the spiritual father is the mother aspect of the deity. And because I don't have a routine mother or father, I've made humanity my mother and father. So when

I run into an elderly woman or even a young woman that brings knowledge to me, she becomes my mother, my teacher."

Red Hawk continued on a spiritual path while starting to explore the visual arts. He worked in oil painting, drawing, and with watercolors. After high school, he focused on graphic arts at Glendale Community College in Arizona. But after only a year and a half of studies, he left school to help care for his mother, who had fallen ill.

Eventually, Red Hawk joined the Navy. He was successful here as well—he was awarded a Navy Achievement Medal for his contribution to training curriculums, and presented a Humanitarian Medal for his role in a heroic rescue of Korean refugees. But his spiritual and artistic nature was calling him back home to Virginia, as were his brothers. They were still living there, and his brothers wanted him to return. "My brothers were screaming at me to come back. They said I had learned everything I could!" His brothers told him, "Look, you're wasting your time! We can get you lecture jobs!" So Red Hawk returned to Virginia and along with his brothers he began working with young audiences. He recalls, "The three of us would do [the talks] together. Black Hawk and I would do storytelling and Swamp Rat would bring his thirteen [stuffed] wolves. Swamp Rat would have six tables of Smithsonian-quality artifacts. He would bring out three or four of them at a time and people would take pictures with the wolves."

Red Hawk, already a seasoned talker who had begun his career telling stories on playgrounds, took to public speaking like a duck to water. "It was old hat to me," said Red Hawk. He was a born communicator, and reaching out to people brought him great joy. He was doing what he loved. "Follow your bliss, follow what's in your heart; if you are a painter, paint. If you love architecture, do architectural stuff, because if you do, you're never going to go wrong. You're always going to be spiritually led because that is your passion. If you do what you love, money will always come because you're passionate."

Red Hawk is proud of his Native American heritage, he says, "I would give up my culture if everyone would just get along . . . I would love to see life without [ethnic] culture—that is, if it meant that there were no wars."

As a Native American speaker, Red Hawk shed new light on racial issues that were not often discussed publicly. It may have been surprising for some to hear that it's not always cool to be an Indian, but that's exactly what Red Hawk spoke about. "Whenever I lecture, and [people] ask me what tribe I belong to, I say 'I used to be Cherokee but I quit.' People say, 'what do you mean, you quit? You can't quit?' I say, 'yeah, I can. I joined the human race'."

Red Hawk continues, "It's not always cool to be an Indian. Native Americans are in the top percentage of every medical dilemma that you can imagine: 110 percent over the national average for diabetes, 115 percent over the national average for incidents of spousal abuse, and the same for alcohol abuse. We are the leaders on just about everything." Native American reservations are often places of great poverty and poor conditions. Because of this, Red Hawk says, "I'd like to see all of the reservations done away with . . . [so that] Native Americans, like all Americans, should be free to pursue their dreams wherever they choose to live." And while Red Hawk is clearly proud of his Native American heritage, he says, "I would give up my culture if everyone would just get along . . . I would love to see life without [ethnic] culture—that is, if it meant that there were no wars."

Red Hawk has a strong opinion on the concept of "Indian Pride." He says, "When people talk to me about Indian Pride,

I say, 'you know, that's your problem. You've got Indian pride, and that pride is your downfall because you exclude yourself from the rest of the world instead of including yourself in the process. You think that fighting the government it is going to give you more rights . . . You can fight it all you want, but the only way you are going to change anything is to get involved and change it from within'."

Red Hawk has spent a lot of time thinking about issues of racism and heritage, and he includes his perspective in his public talks. He says, "If your heritage—be it Celtic or African American or Indian—if your heritage prevents you from being included in the rest of the world, then you have to stop and take a look at what's important to you. If you're saying, 'My Indian heritage is more important than [the heritage of] this guy sitting next to me, this white guy who put me down and stole my land'—if that's your attitude toward him, then that's a prideful attitude [and] your heritage is holding you back."

But Red Hawk does not stop with a discussion of racial issues. He uses his speaking engagements to teach about spiritual and cultural differences. He believes that all races and all cultures deserve to know about Native American spirituality. "I don't believe in this sacredness . . . [which] is only for me and not for you. Because if it is the same God, with the same energy and same information, why wouldn't you want to share? If we are saying that the white man has this philosophy of 'rape the land, move and displace everything' at the rule of the government, isn't it our duty to enlighten them? If we have information that will make them better people, so that they don't do to us what they've done to other people, isn't it our responsibility to share that information? I don't think sacredness belongs to any one particular person. If you have information, give it to people. If I took you under my wing for a year and taught you everything I know about spiritual and cultural concepts, what have I lost? I still know what I know. But what will you have gained from it? You will have been enlightened ten times over, and I still know what I know."

Red Hawk's reputation as a public speaker gained national recognition. Red Hawk traveled extensively and spoke at many schools, and to corporations and federal agencies on concepts such as diversity, racism, and multicultural training. On one of his travels, Red Hawk met his future wife. He recalls, "My wife was doing a paper on Native American culture at Brigham Young University [in Provost, Utah]. She interviewed me and we hit it off."

Red Hawk's notoriety as a speaker and spiritual leader continued to grow. He received a call from the Chief of the American Cherokee Confederacy (ACC) in Georgia, a Cherokee organization with members from all over the United States. Red Hawk was asked to be clan chief for the Utah, Arizona and Nevada district states and also to serve on the tribal council as their Spiritual Leader. Red Hawk had always tried to stay away from Indian politics, so it was difficult to persuade him to accept the offer. Eventually he agreed.

Within his first few months as spiritual leader, Red Hawk was overwhelmed with complaints. "You talk about phone calls and e-mails! Some of the most bickering stuff: 'someone touched my eagle feather, that's not right! Someone said something about somebody, he's an elder, and that's not right!' I thought, 'Are you such children that you have to come to me with these things?' I can imagine how Christ was—not that I put myself in his realm, but in trying to teach people. I'm trying to teach people about the higher concept of spirituality and they are worried about physical objects. It's not about symbolism, it's about your intentions, and it's about the heart. When you do sweat lodges, when you do vision quests, the purpose is to get in contact with something higher than yourself. If you get tied up in the symbolism, you're never going to get beyond the symbolism."

After six months as Spiritual Leader, the Chief asked Red Hawk to help kick out some members of the tribe with whom he had some personal differences. Red Hawk didn't agree with the Chief and wouldn't help. They had an argument, and then Red Hawk resigned. Four months later, the tribal council kicked out the Chief. The tribe fell apart and eventually lost their status as a state-recognized tribe.

Assistant Chief Eagle Eye Burk called Red Hawk and asked him to lead the disbanded tribe. Red Hawk agreed and took over the reins as Principal Chief. Since the Cherokee Confederacy had lost its state status, Red Hawk helped to create the new United Cherokee Nation (UNC), a formal membership organization and corporation. "We still get backlash," he says. "We are not saying we are a tribe. We are a Cherokee membership organization." As Chief and President of the United Cherokee Nation, Red Hawk hopes to unite the Cherokee people and increase its membership. It has Clan Chiefs in nearly all fifty states, and these are overseen by Chief District Leaders and a panel of tribal elders, and ultimately by Chief Red Hawk.

Red Hawk's perspective on belonging to any group or organization is interesting. Many people think they need to belong to a group to gain strength, but Red Hawk looks at it differently. "I'm not a big proponent of belonging to groups or organizations in order to make a point or become strong. I think you have to become strong first. If you're looking for an organization to make you strong, then you'll get a bunch of weak people joined together. You've got to be strong to change the world."

Red Hawk has achieved the kind of success that few people will ever know, yet he remains humble. He believes that for all people the process of personal growth never ends. And he says that there is always someone to share your knowledge with. "I realize that for every time I climb to the top of a tree, I can look up and see a taller tree. And just when you think you know it all, guess what? You start back at the bottom and there's an even higher tree. But when I look down, I can see all those little saplings growing, and other people working their way up."

It's a sure thing for anyone climbing their way up, that the wisdom and support of Chief Red Hawk will be there to help.

Chief Red Hawk lives in Richmond, Virginia with his wife and daughter. He loves to say to his daughter: *"Namaste."* Pronounced Nahm-as-tay), this is an ancient Sanskrit word which means something like, "the spirit in me greets and honors the spirit in you." And as a successful public speaker, artist, storyteller, writer, and musician, the spirit of Chief Red Hawk has already greeted the spirit of well over a million people.

Red Hawk has written and self-published two books of prose, *The Tao of an Indian* and *A Course in Diversity*. In *The Tao of an Indian* he translates Taoist principles—an ancient Chinese philosophy—to apply to American Indian beliefs. Because he is skilled in both graphic design and writing, Red Hawk created the book from start to finish. He has also written books of poetry, and released CDs entitled *Flight of the Hawk* and *The Songs Remember*. Check them out!

The best leaders are those who people scarcely know exist.

The next best leader is a leader who is cherished and praised.

Next comes the one who is feared.

The worst one is a leader who is despised.

The best leaders value their words, and use them sparingly.

If a leader does not trust the people he guides, the people will become untrustworthy.

When leaders accomplish their task, the people should be made to feel that they did it, all by themselves.

"The Tao of an Indian"
—*Red Hawk*

Larry Merculieff

COMMUNITY LEADER

How much is one person capable of accomplishing? Well, if you're Larry Merculieff, who has a remarkably long list of triumphs, the answer is "a lot!" Larry, an Aleut from Saint Paul Island, has been committed to bringing his once-oppressed people to a new position of power and self-sufficiency. His home and birthplace of Saint Paul Island is a thriving community, due in part to his commitment and efforts.

Saint Paul Island is one of the Pribolof Islands, a series of wild and beautiful volcanic islands in the Bering Sea, south-west of Alaska. This group of islands is known as the "Galapagos of the North" because of the diversity of wildlife, especially birds, which live there. It is also called "The Birth-place of the Wind" which tells you something about the

challenging climate. "It's really a magical place," says Larry. "The island I was born and raised on is 5 miles (8 km) wide and 12 miles (19 km) long. There are one million northern fur seals, 2.5 million seabirds, one thousand reindeer and five hundred Aleut people. My people have been out in the Bering Sea for about ten thousand years and we're still here although our numbers have diminished substantially."

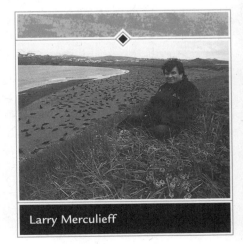

Larry Merculieff

According to Larry, the people of his generation are the last to have received a completely traditional upbringing. At age four, the last living Aleut medicine man gave Larry his traditional name, Kuuyux, which means "extension"—as in "the extension between ancient knowledge and modern time," a bridge between the past and the present. Among Larry's people, only one person holds the name Kuuyux in each lifetime. The medicine man had held that name until he passed it on to Larry.

At age five, Larry encountered an Aleut elder who would mentor him throughout his life. They entered into a traditional Aachaa relationship. Larry explains, "An Aachaa relationship is a profound relationship. It is not established by virtue of family ties or anything like that. You don't just go out and pick your Aachaa, it just happens organically. The older person and the younger person see each other and you just know that's your Aachaa. Nick Stepedin (Larry's Aachaa) was a very, very wise man. He taught me much of what I know about being an Aleut, and being a man, but most importantly about relationships...with myself, with the land, with the sea, animals and other people. Yet from when I was age five to age thirteen, he literally may have said two hundred words to me. There is a lot of wisdom in that way of teaching. Words are not only superfluous, but they diminish one's own ability to experience."

Larry's Aachaa taught him to hunt and to have reverence for all forms of life. As a young boy, Larry was expected to sit near the shoreline with his Aachaa and wait for the sea lions to come. "My job was to simply watch. It was never explained, I was simply expected to watch." After many hours of waiting and watching, Larry would often find himself zoning out and becoming entranced with the rhythm of the ocean. He noticed, though, that none of the older men in the tribe were doing this. Later, through his own explorations, Larry would come to understand what this meant.

When he was only six, Larry was able to roam and explore on his own on Saint Paul Island. "One of the interesting aspects of my traditional upbringing is that I was given a range of freedom that very few children have today. I could go anywhere I wanted, any time, day or night. I didn't have a curfew. I was left to explore anything I wanted to explore. I could go to anyone's house day or night and I was welcomed like a long lost son. I would be affirmed every day by every adult for years; I was never scolded."

Left on his own to explore, Larry would wake up at 4 a.m. and walk for miles in either direction. One of his favorite activities was to visit the large bird cliffs near the shoreline. Millions of sea birds slept on the shore cliffs and Larry would walk out to watch them as they woke. At sunrise the birds would awaken, and thousands and thousands of birds would swoop and fly along the cliff ledges, sometimes within inches of Larry. On one day in particular, he discovered a connection in the teachings of his Aachaa. "One day it struck me that these birds never collided with each other, but they were concentrated in front of these cliffs by the thousands. They

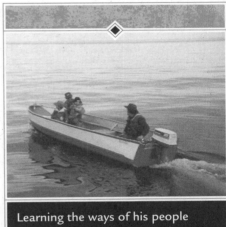

Learning the ways of his people through his Aachaa was an important part of Larry's education.

were flying at different speeds, heights, and directions and yet they did not even clip a wing." Larry realized that day that there is a connection between the flight of the birds and why the men of his tribe did not zone out from the rhythm of the water when they were watching for the seals. He describes his revelation: "I saw that the birds were intensely present in the moment. They knew in advance where they needed to go. I decided to try this, and when I would sit out on the rocks [watching for the sea lions], I would try to mimic the birds as best as I could. By staying present and not allowing my mind to drift, not using my thoughts because birds don't use thought, I was never lulled again."

Learning the ways of his people through his Aachaa was not Larry's only form of education. At about this same time, Larry was forced—like many other Native children—to attend a government-regulated boarding school. As with most government-run residential schools, Native children were forced to follow strict guidelines. Larry lived in an army barracks-style open dormitory with forty other boys from different Alaskan communities. In military style, they were forced awake at 6 a.m. to do chores. They were only permitted to see their families in the summertime and were allowed to write very few letters. At Christmas, Larry was allowed to have a short conversation with his family on a two-way radio. Larry remembers, "It was a pretty stunted way to communicate, because we would talk like a ham-radio operator: 'Yeah, I'm doing okay. Over!' But still, it meant a lot to know our parents were still there and that they were okay. The hardest times were the holidays like Christmas; we would sit in the barracks and remember the joyous festivities that used to happen on the island." Sadly, Larry and his classmates called the government-run institution "the school without love."

But Larry managed to survive year after year and eventually he advanced to the upper school. However, he continually met with more rules and regulations that fueled his rebellious nature. In the upper school, the students were more closely watched. Although they were allowed to participate in a few social activities like school dances, they were required to maintain a definite distance from the girls. And they were certainly not allowed to give a girl a simple goodnight kiss.

Larry's frustration at being watched and monitored provoked him into action. He organized a petition that stated: "We the undersigned students at Mt. Edgecumbe High School demand to be treated as young adults and have a meaningful voice in the rules and regulations that govern us." All six hundred students signed the petition, and Larry

Merculieff, at age fifteen, bravely marched into the superintendent's office and delivered it. He did not know what to expect, and he feared expulsion. As it turned out, however, the superintendent was a compassionate man who respected Larry's courage, and instead he invited him to dinner.

The superintendent said to Larry, "You think you can do this responsibly? Okay, I'll give you a blank check and the student council can make the rules and regulations for the student body, including the conduct in the dormitories." Larry says, "I thought, 'Wow, that's really great.' I went to the student council and asked for the first new rule to be that we could kiss our boyfriends and girlfriends good night. And it passed! I was voted the first honorary president of the girl's dormitory. I became the most popular boy in school, and when I ran for student body president the following year, I won by an awkward landslide. I felt sorry for the other guy—he got three votes, and I got all the rest."

Larry continued in high school and graduated in 1966, at age sixteen. At graduation, he was faced with an important decision. Previously, all Aleut tribal men were required to attend school until the age of sixteen and then they had to work in a job for the government. But Larry had graduated at an interesting and exciting time in the history of his community. The Aleutian people were in the process of negotiating and obtaining some measures of freedom from government control that they had not experienced in centuries.

In order to appreciate what this meant for the Aleutian people, it is necessary to understand some of their history.

In the late 1700s, Russian fur hunters landed on the Aleutian Islands. The islands were teeming with otters, walrus, seals, sea lions, whales, and billions of sea birds. They invaded the islands, imprisoned the people who had lived there for centuries, and forced the Aleutian people to kill enormous numbers of animals for fur. They were forced to kill thirty to forty thousand seals in one year, wiping out the seal population, so the Aleut people were left to fend for themselves during the winter. This mass enslavement—which caused widespread starvation and disease—led to an eighty percent decrease in the Aleutian population over a fifty-year period. It was known as "The time of the great death." There are many tales of the horrors that the Aleutian people faced, including a grim story of how, on one occasion, the Russians placed bets on how many Aleutians could be killed with one musket ball—their large and deadly bullets. They lined up the men and shot, killing nine.

The Russians maintained this system of slavery until 1867, when the United States purchased Alaska and its territorial islands. As Larry states, "People always say the U.S. 'bought Alaska.' We say they bought the rights to jurisdiction of these lands illegally. The indigenous people were not consenting."

When the U.S. took over in 1867, the government managed the islands for the same purposes as the Russians and maintained the Aleutians as a captive labor force. The Aleutians were forced to live under U.S rule, which included living in government-built wooden homes. They were accustomed to living in traditional homes that were built half underground and that were partially warmed with the natural heat of the earth. Unlike their traditional homes, the new wooden houses were not insulated and nearly impossible to heat in the harsh Alaskan winters. Residents were issued only one blanket per bed and the houses were heated with government-issued (and restricted) coal.

In World War II, Japan invaded the Aleutian chain of islands. Fearing an Aleut uprising, the U.S. military moved the Aleut people to internment camps in abandoned food canneries. At one internment camp, 380 men, women, and children (including elders) were dropped off with only two crates of dry bread. The military assumed the Aleutians would be able to survive in the elements and so left them to fend for themselves. However, the area was much different from where they had always lived. They lost at least ten percent of their population to malnutrition and disease. Larry

Merculieff's mother was among those who suffered in the internment camps.

When the Aleutians were returned to their homes after the war, they found that their houses had been ransacked, all their valuables had been stolen, and their churches were gutted. Some Aleutians were placed in one of the larger communities within the Aleutian island chain, never to see their villages or homes again.

The government continued to control these communities: salaries were paid with food vouchers and government-issue clothing rather than money because the military feared the Aleut people would use money to leave the island. All mail was censored. No group gatherings or assemblies were allowed. Protests against this treatment were dealt with harshly, with loss of job or deportation off the island and away from family. "My people never knew what is was like to be free, we didn't have anything to compare it to. We were completely isolated from the rest of the world. So we say, 'like the Jews, we had our holocaust; like the Japanese, we were interned; like the Africans, we were enslaved.'"

Since the government did not allow the Aleutians to congregate, the Aleutians had to devise clever plans to enable gatherings. They came up with the idea of putting on plays for government personnel, and they used their planning and rehearsal time to have secret meetings. Through these meetings they put together letters that they smuggled off the island to the editor of a large Alaskan Native newspaper. An article was written exposing the atrocities against the Aleutian people and in 1965 there was a congressional investigation. In 1966 an Alaskan Bill of Rights—similar to a constitution—was developed, and the Aleutian people were finally given back freedoms that they had not known for almost two hundred years. It was in the midst of tasting this new freedom that Larry Merculieff decided to go to college.

Even though a Bill of Rights declared that the Aleut people had new rights and freedoms, they still often met with resistance. Larry met with a school counselor about going to college. Instead of supportive encouragement, the counselor suggested that Larry should attend a small school because he assumed he would have a better chance of succeeding there. Larry wouldn't hear of it. Out of sheer determination and rebellious defiance, Larry chose the biggest school he could find on the west coast, the University of Washington (U of W) in Seattle, which had a student population of more than 34,000. Larry, who had been brought up in a community of a few hundred people, was in for a shock. He remembers, "When I got to U of W, I didn't know what I was doing. I didn't even know how to take a bus. I had no idea how large classes were going to be; in fact, I had no idea what college was. But my people had been encouraging me ever since I was a little kid. They'd say, 'One day you're going to go out and get an education, and then you're going to come back and help our people.' I got to U of W, I went to my first class, and it was practically as big as my entire village. I couldn't believe it! Classes as big as three hundred and four hundred students, all in one lecture room. That was incredible culture shock."

At age seventeen, in a world miles away and enormously different from the one he had grown up in, Larry managed to make it through his first year of college. He returned to the island for the summer and immediately the Tribal Council asked to meet with him and another tribal member who had also gone away to college.

As the fourth person in the history of his people to go to college, Larry and the other student were asked to help implement an independent government for his island. He would serve as a representative for his tribe and travel across the country to Washington D.C. to seek assistance. At age seventeen, Larry Merculieff would be helping to create a brand new city.

Larry's experience in Washington was invigorating. "I made the mistake of renting a car," he remembers. "It took me six hours to go twenty miles, and I got seventeen parking tickets! But I was there with all the inspiration and determination of my people so I was never afraid. They had taught me that nothing was impossible."

Larry and his companion met with Alaska's congressman Ted Stevens, who took a liking to the young men from Saint Paul Island. He was impressed by the gutsy actions of the two and their passionate vision for their people, and he agreed to help. Larry was able to secure fifty thousand dollars to help start the city of St. Paul. "We actually created a city in 1971!" he recalls proudly.

After returning to the University of Washington the following year, Larry did research and discovered that in a school of more than 34,000 students, only four identified themselves as Native American, even though there were twenty-two Indian reservations in Washington State alone.

Once again Larry found himself with a mission, and once again he bravely marched into the school administrator's office—this time the President of the University. Larry did not have an appointment and was told the president was too busy. But Larry was persistent and eventually found himself sitting in the president's office. "I go in there and tell him my story about the twenty-two Indian reservations, 34,000 students at U of W and only four Native Americans. He didn't have to think about it for very long. He said, 'Okay, you can be in charge of bringing more Native Americans to the University.'"

Larry was appointed to a brand new position within the University—he became the Recruiter and Financial Aid Advisor of Native People. He was given a budget and use of a state car to travel to the reservations. Not bad for an eighteen-year-old! In addition, Larry started the Indian Education Program at the University of Washington, which today is an entire university department.

Larry continued his college education at U of W, while reaching out to other Native students. His successes were widely recognized and he was asked to join other Native

American organizations such as the National Indian Educational Advisory Board and The Convocation of American Indian Scholars. He was also named Chairperson of a committee that investigated allegations of abuse within Native schools.

Larry eventually graduated from university, and was soon offered a job to develop a link between the Aleutian villages and the University system. He successful prepared a grant application and was awarded $600,000 dollars for the betterment of the Aleutian people.

The President of the Aleut Corporation then hired him after openly arguing with him during a meeting. He recalls, "I thought he would never talk to me again, but he said he liked it, and he hired me on the spot."

Larry was appointed Director of the Land Department of the Aleut Corporation. He met with Aleutian Island village leaders to determine what lands they wanted to lay claim to under a new program of compensation for lands lost to the U.S. Government. He visited the islands on a seaplane. It was dangerous travel in a place with unpredictable weather and often stormy seas, but the operation was a success. "We surveyed two thousand islands, we sat with the elders to ask what was important to them—What do you use? Where are your graveyards? Where are your historical sites? Our corporation was the only one of twelve [Native organizations] that did not have any legal challenges to our land claims. I was probably the first Aleut to ever visit every Aleut village."

In 1975, Larry was asked to fulfill a lifelong dream of giving back to his Native community. "St. Paul asked if I would be their business manager and start up the first private enterprise on the island." The first businesses he decided to launch were a boat harbor on the island and an eco-tourism operation. "With a million seals and 2.5 million sea birds, we figured we would be a mecca for eco-tourists."

A government building was soon converted to a hotel, and Larry approached the tourism project with the needs of his community in mind. "I went to the community and said that we are not going to do anything that the people don't want, and we are going to do it according to our cultural way."

He based the tourism plans on the wishes of his community, and with special regard for the concerns of the elders. No dogs would be allowed on the island, for example, because they disturbed the seals. No rifles or firearms would be permitted. Tourists could not interfere with the lifestyle of the community. No camping was allowed on the island and all visitors were to be escorted by a guide.

The approach worked beautifully and Larry's eco-tourism plan was a huge success. The environment remained intact, the community was pleased, and the tourists, mindful of the conditions of their visits, were eager to comply. And because of the success of the eco-tourism trade, the boat harbor was successfully constructed.

Larry eventually became President of the St. Paul Village Corporation. "Today the St. Paul Village Corporation is still following the original principles [of respect for the community's wishes]. They have put up giant wind turbine generators for eventual energy self-sufficiency. They are working on a hydroponics operation (growing vegetables and plants using nutrient-rich solutions and controlled lighting) to raise their own food. The St. Paul Village Corporation is successful. When I started, the budget was $300,000; when I left, it was worth $9 million. Now it is worth over $23 million."

In 1995, Larry had a vision in which his Aachaa told him to leave the island. Larry heeded the vision and began once again to reach out to other Native communities. This time, though, it was a spiritual quest he was undertaking.

He met with many tribes including the Lakota and Hopi from the U.S., the Stony Elders from Alberta, the Maori people of New Zealand, and the Mapuche from Chile, in South America. Larry was treated as a guest of honor at his meetings with the tribal elders. He was asked to be a messenger, and invited to take part in sacred ceremonies. At one particular Maori ceremony, in which all of the people were

Larry is treated as a guest of honor at meetings with the tribal elders the world over. He is a considered a messenger and is invited to take part in sacred ceremonies.

speaking in their Native language, an elder stopped and turned to Larry. He surprised him by saying, in English, "We know why you have come." The elder continued, "Many people feel like they have lost their ways." Larry watched, transfixed. He recalls, "They were smoking from the sacred pipes, and the pipes were spaced four feet apart in a circular form, but the smoke all moved to the center and created a spiral, like a rope being kneaded together."

The elder continued to speak, "We have been praying to the creator and we have a message for you to carry back. Your ways have not been lost, the ways of many of our people have never been lost, they have been kept for you in the unseen world, waiting for you to wake up in spirit." The elder finished speaking and Larry was overwhelmed. "That was the end of it, and that statement went right through my heart. It was such a profound spiritual experience for me."

Larry continued to meet with elders of many tribes, including a woman in Chile named Rosa, a 126-year-old Mapuche woman. During one ceremony, Rosa read the sacred ceremonies for four days straight from 6 a.m. to 1 a.m. with only a small break to eat.

Larry returned to St. Paul and shared the messages he had received from the elders, especially from the Maori. He was warmly received and people were eager to hear his stories. "When I returned," he says, "I got a call to emcee a concert by the Indigo Girls! In the concert hall were two thousand people that wanted me to share. So I shared the story of the Maori elders. In one year, I must have spoken to over forty thousand people. It was amazing how all the doors opened up."

Today, Larry Merculieff continues to spread his spiritual message and takes every opportunity to speak out, especially to young people. He lives up to his name—Kuuyux—and is indeed a bridge between generations. His message is inspiring:

"It is the time of great change, to reconnect to the great sacredness within ourselves, to know what it is that we must do. All of the sacred colors—red, white, black and yellow—have within them the knowledge and wisdom of our ancestors. In order to access that knowledge and wisdom, you've got to go into your own healing, you've got to go deep inside yourself. The elders say you cannot offer the world that which you do not have. If I choose to do something to help in this world, I've got to help myself first. The most unselfish act is to focus on your own healing, to become aware as a real human being, to be fully present in order to receive the guidance of all that is divine, so that you'll know what you'll need to do no matter what your life challenges are. Those who remain disconnected from this

Larry Merculieff continues to spread his spiritual message and takes every opportunity to speak out, especially to young people. He lives up to his name—Kuuyux—and is indeed a bridge between generations.

sacredness within them will be lost. I have the highest hope for young people to achieve this in a way they haven't been able to in this generation. It has been prophesized that young people are again going to speak with the wisdom of elders during this time."

Larry has served on numerous boards, forums and committees and has spoken widely on environmental concerns

The ancient Aleutians, according to anthropological accounts, were an amazing people. The young men, in order to prepare themselves to become seaworthy, would run up and down steep hills with large stones held outstretched at arm's length. They would place themselves in freezing ocean waters in the winter and practice staying for longer and longer periods of time without suffering from frostbite. The ancient Aleuts were also known to have performed a type of brain surgery, and had a word in their language that represented the number one billion.

in the Alaskan and other northern regions. He was a co-director of the Alaska Region of the Native American Fish and Wildlife Society, and is the cofounder of the Indigenous Peoples Council for Marine Mammals (where he served as chairman), the Alaska Oceans Network, and the Alaska Forum on the Environment. He now serves as the Deputy Director of the Alaska Native Science Commission, and hopes one day to write a book on the history of the Aleut people.

Through incredible commitment, courage, and determination, Larry Merculieff—Kuuyux—has achieved much in his lifetime, and serves as a great inspiration to the Aleutian people, to Native communities worldwide, and to all people.

Chief Frank Abraham

LITTLE BLACK RIVER FIRST NATION

Every so often a heroic figure arrives just in time to make a valiant rescue. When the Little Black River Ojibwe band on the eastern shores of Lake Winnipeg was in serious trouble, Frank Abraham turned up to provide service, wisdom and honesty. He made decisions and created opportunities that enabled his band to rise up

Frank Abraham

out of near financial failure, and helped to bring a sense of pride and accomplishment to his people.

Frank Abraham was born in 1955. His family was poor and he lived the first years of his life in a one-room shack with his mother and grandparents. Possibly to help overcome these challenges, Frank became rooted in the strong spiritual teachings of his people. His Ojibwe name is Neewin Enokawen Kacaa Keepote, which translates as "Four Directions Speaker." The four directions are 1) to understand one's self, 2) to understand spirituality, 3) to understand the reasons for living and 4) to understand the importance of giving to others. According to the Ojibwe, by following these four directions a person comes to understand how all things in life are related and fit together. Frank has followed the meaning of his name throughout the course of his life, in his struggles to understand who he is and what he thinks is right, and how he can be of service to his people.

When Frank was five years old, he was forced to leave his family to go live in an Indian boarding school far from his village and band. At that time, the Government of Canada believed that Native children should be removed from their families, forced to forget their Native language and be educated in English. The school, which was run by Indian and Northern Affairs Canada (INAC), was in a remote area; Frank had to travel first by boat, then by train, and finally by bus to get there. Leaving his home and family was painful for Frank and it was made worse by the knowledge that he wouldn't be allowed to go home for Christmas. He remembers, "It was very tough [to say goodbye to my mother]. When you got on the bus, you didn't know if you were ever coming home again. It was scary."

Frank was very unhappy at the boarding school and soon found that he was struggling to hold on to his Native identity. The teachers were stern and their strict rules forbid the children from doing anything connected to their Native heritage. His memories of those days are painful:

"We were in a school that was all aboriginal, [but we] were not allowed to speak our language; every time we spoke it we were punished. My teacher was so mean at times. She wouldn't allow children to use the bathroom and would rub their noses in their urine if they couldn't hold it. She would yell, 'Why did you do that? Why didn't you tell me?' It was terrible."

Frank struggled to learn English in school; the methods were unconventional and the teacher was not sympathetic to a young Ojibwe. "I grew up speaking my language. [But at the school] if we could not pronounce a word (in English), she would hit us right in the knuckles with a ruler. She wouldn't use the flat side; she'd use the edge side. Some of the words were ones we were hearing for the first time. We didn't know; we didn't understand. It was very tough."

Although the school made it almost impossible, an important person in Frank's life helped him to hold on to his Ojibwe identity. This person was his grandfather, John Richard Bird. Frank says that, "my Grandfather was very prominent in my life, and in understanding who I was. It wasn't until much later that I began to understand what he meant. I think it was through his teachings and wisdom that I was able to maintain my own identity."

According to family relatives, John's grandfather lived until between 106 and 109 years old. He was respected within the Native community and held fast to his beliefs. One of Frank's most important memories is of how his grandfather helped to save Frank's younger brother's life. "When my brother was nine years old, he had meningitis. The hospital gave him six months to live. They asked my mother if they wanted to keep him in the hospital. My Grandfather said 'What's the use if you're going to give up on him, we'll take him home.' They gave him medicines and healed my brother. Frank was greatly influenced by the strength and actions of his grandfather, and this influence enabled him to survive the difficulties of school.

Fortunately for Frank and the other students, the school was not open year-round. He could return to his family and village in the summers to busy himself with normal boyhood activities. Although his family was poor, Frank was resourceful; "We never really had anything. To get a bike, I used to have to go to the garbage dump and build a bike of my own. It would make you creative."

Even though Frank was always happy to return to his home, he was not always warmly welcomed. Some of his own band people began to turn their backs on him. "People treated you differently, people looked at you differently. I remember one of the great aunts telling one of her adopted boys that he couldn't play with me anymore because I was going to boarding school. That sticks out in my mind [because] she went through boarding school herself. You weren't welcomed into a household like you used to be before you left. Before I would just walk in, [but after] when I tried to walk in people would say, 'why don't you knock before you come in, eh?'"

Frank's life as a young aboriginal became confusing. He continued school, where he was treated poorly regardless of how hard he tried. And now his own people looked at him differently, though the reasons were not always clear to him. "Aboriginal people sometimes become very funny. There is a division within our own people at times, whether they have status or non-status, or whether they divide themselves into Métis or First Nations. This is sometimes reflected in how we look at other people. For some reason I felt that in the community perspective I wasn't fully accepted by everybody."

Frank's mother remarried and the family moved to a mining town where his stepfather found a job. After Frank finished school, he followed in the footsteps of his stepfather and became a miner. He enjoyed the work and was talented at mining and easily gained respect from his supervisors and co-workers. "I worked in the mines for about twelve years. It was one of the first real jobs I ever had. I loved it because I traveled through the country quite a bit, through Canada from Ontario to the Northwest Territories. I worked for gold mines and I was very good at what I did.".

Frank became so efficient at his trade that he was often able to work for two hours to accomplish what would take most people a full day. He was rewarded with extra bonuses. "I worked in one area in Northern British Columbia. I worked by myself, which was rare. I drilled, loaded and blasted three 8x10-foot areas in one shift. It gave me a sense of accomplishment. I could be the best at what I wanted to do. I could achieve what I wanted to achieve. I was good at it."

Mining, however, is a dangerous profession. Underground, miners are faced with the possibility of life-threatening accidents such as explosions, cave-ins, or falling down deep mineshafts. Frank eventually grew weary of the danger. He had lost a friend in a mining accident, and saw many mishaps on the job. In one situation, Frank and a partner were working together above a deep opening. Frank suggested to his partner that he wear a safety belt, and just as he finished his sentence, his partner fell headfirst down the long drop. Luckily, his partner managed to grab a ladder on the way down but still badly injured his shoulder. Frank immediately climbed down the ladder and carried his partner (who, according to Frank was no lightweight!) to safety.

After Frank finished school, he followed in the footsteps of his stepfather and became a miner.

Another time, a less experienced miner leaned out of a moving cage elevator and got his head lodged. Frank yelled in time to stop the elevator then used a steel rod to bend back the thick bar, which allowed the miner to free himself. Frank's quick actions saved the young man's life. However, the next day the miner was fired and

Frank was reprimanded. That was all that Frank needed; he quit mining and returned to the Ojibwe community.

Back in his community, Frank became interested in band matters and began to attend meetings. He soon learned of the frustration among his people with the governing band council. "I learned how disgruntled they were (due to) the lack of information on how decisions were made. I became involved."

Soon after his decision to be more involved, Frank was appointed assistant administrator for the Ojibwe band. He had self-taught himself management and accounting skills by reading and studying books. After he was appointed to the council position he began taking formal business courses. Aided by this new knowledge, Frank noticed something peculiar about the band's financial records. Many transactions did not seem legitimate. According to Frank, "They were all lining their pockets pretty thick. It was band money. We ran into financial problems for the community, and it was tough to make ends meet."

Frank, who was not yet in a position to take action against his superiors, watched with dismay as the band's money was mismanaged. Finally, he could not hold his tongue any longer. In a brave move that could have jeopardized his own position, Frank chose to speak his conscience at a public meeting. "I couldn't live with it any more. It was uncomfortable for me and I just couldn't let it pass. At the first opportunity, I just blurted out to the community members exactly what was going on."

The accusation of mismanagement was met with outrage from people at the meeting. He was accusing leadership officials of stealing and some of these leaders and their family members were relatives of Frank. "They actually thought I was the bad seed and [I was] the one that was doing it. It was a big name-calling thing. I wrote in a journal [before the meeting] about the reaction I was going to get. I was right. People were calling me a person of the forked tongue.

I didn't really understand band politics [then] because I hadn't really lived there. I had all my facts down and all my info there; the council couldn't argue against me. I thought I would lose my job."

In the following election, not only did Frank keep his job, but he was also nominated for a council position. His family had always been leaders and now it was Frank's turn to carry on the tradition. In the newly elected council, Frank's first cousin was chief and Frank was in charge of money. "I kept a close eye on the finances. I would red-circle the questionable transactions to let one of the council members know I was watching. One day when the chief was away and I was left as the acting chief, I caught [the thief]. I said, 'Listen, I can't trust you, but I don't have the authority to fire you. I'm going to send you home [and] I'll talk to the chief. You'll present your arguments and then the decision will be made.' He never did show up."

In the new council, as a way of demonstrating their fiscal responsibility, one of the most important policies to be implemented was a rule that no one could receive financial advances. This was not well received by the band; however, the council was determined to stick by it and lead by example. The council members did not take advances for themselves either.

Despite their best efforts, financial troubles arose in the first year of the new council. By November, the band was short of money and would not be receiving any assistance until the following April. They struggled but managed to survive through the year. "We had to do some creative financing . . . from payday to payday we didn't know if we were going to make payroll or not."

By the second year, although things were still tough, the council began to see some improvement. They did not run short of money until after Christmas, and the council was becoming more open to members of the community. One of the many concerns of the Ojibwe community was the quality of their housing. They had no indoor plumbing, which left them reliant on outhouses and shared community water faucets. With Frank's guidance, the council was able to secure government funding to install plumbing and water hook-ups in eight homes. However, Frank had a more ambitious plan that he shared with the chief. He suggested, "Instead of bringing contractors into the community, let's utilize our people. We'll buy (construction) machines; we have machine operators in the community. Let's use them."

At the next band meeting, the chief informed the community of the new funding that would allow work to begin right away. He then informed everyone that Frank had an idea and perhaps they should listen to him. Frank described the process: Instead of paying the money directly to a contractor, the band would use it to purchase equipment and pay a contractor to help train the Ojibwe people. Frank admitted there would be a learning period, but if in the future there were ever problems with the plumbing, they would have the equipment and knowledge to fix them themselves.

The band was convinced. Following Frank's plan proved to be a smart financial decision. They band successfully equipped the eight houses that the government had funded with indoor plumbing, as well as eight additional ones. Not only had they used the same amount of money that was designated for eight units, but also the Ojibwe had also provided valuable training for their people and now owned construction equipment for future projects and repairs. To the delight of band people needing work, most of the money stayed within the community, creating jobs and paying their wages. The creative mindset of Frank Abraham had established a true win-win situation for the council, the band and the community.

The following year, Frank distributed the Council's annual financial report to the entire Ojibwe community. Previously this report was given only to the Department of Indian Affairs; however, the Band Council—acting on their commitment to more openness—made sure that the report was given to everyone. Not surprisingly, the report was well received.

While Frank was increasing his involvement with band council matters, the Chief was decreasing his involvement and the Acting Chief was becoming more and more involved with his own small business. Frank expressed his concern to the Chief that band matters were being neglected. In the next council elections both Frank and the Chief were nominated. Respectfully, Frank offered to step down if the Chief intended to run for the position; however, wanting the best for his people, the Chief unselfishly withdrew his name from the election. As a result, Frank became chief of the Ojibwe people.

Within two weeks of his appointment, Frank was sent to Geneva, Switzerland, as an ambassador to the annual meeting of the United Nations Working Group on Indigenous Populations. There, he helped fight for the Ojibwe's right to be called a People as opposed to an organization. The fight was ultimately successful, and in 1997 the band became formally recognized as a People with the further possibility of being recognized as a Nation.

On his return home, Frank began negotiations for a water and sewer project that would provide plumbing to additional households in the Ojibwe community. Initially, the Canadian government was offering a less-expensive low-pressure system that would cost 1.2 million dollars. After speaking extensively with engineers, Frank decided that a ground-flow system would be more beneficial for his people. The three million dollar price tag was a problem but Frank knew about money. After careful research, he discovered that the cheaper low-pressure system would be more expensive in the long run due to costly upkeep and maintenance. In a meeting with representatives from Indian and Northern Affairs, Frank argued his point. INAC fought against his ideas but in the end, Frank's arguments were so well thought-out and persuasive that the INAC engineers came to his defense. Frank won and the band was awarded the funds for the additional water and sewer projects.

When the time came to initiate the project, Frank once again demonstrated his honesty and courage. When awarded the money, many contractors came to offer their services in hopes of getting the contract. One contractor offered to pay each of the council members thirty thousand dollars in hopes of getting the contract. Frank says, "We pointed him to the road!"

When the funding came through, Frank's house was still without plumbing. Once again Frank choose to forego his own needs and put his people first by ordering work to begin on other community members' houses. And once again, a contractor would be used to provide training to the band and they would do most of the work themselves.

At the groundbreaking ceremony for the project, the director of INAC learned that the band leaders, including Chief Frank Abraham, had put themselves last on the list to receive indoor plumbing. The director was impressed. Two weeks later, Frank received a phone call from INAC and learned that in addition to the original water and sewer project, they were to be awarded funding for a low-pressure system for the remainder of the houses in the community, including the council members.

Frank gladly accepted the additional funding and although he could have rested there, he continued to work for the best deal for his people. "By utilizing the best efforts and negotiating for the best deals, I was able to purchase all the tubs and toilet bowls for every household at a reasonable price. We outfitted all the houses. We made a profit! We were able to build our community center without a dime from INAC!"

Frank Abraham not only helped to bring his band out of a financial disaster, but he also helped to provide training, education and self-sufficiency to his people. His actions were honorable and unselfish. He is a heroic man worthy of holding the title of chief.

Frank Abraham with his wife, Rhonda and four of their eleven children.

Today, Frank Abraham has moved on from his position of Chief of the Black River First Nation, and he now works in Winnipeg for a Child Welfare Agency Program. He wants to set an example for upcoming generations and offers these words of advice: "It goes back to my understanding of who I am as a person. The whole idea behind my name—the four directions—has so many meanings. [The name] teaches you about who you are as an individual, and it teaches you respect, caring, understanding and honesty. It comes to an understanding of what love is all about."

Frank is eager to share his philosophy and the rules that helped him through the most challenging times in his life: "When you love yourself, you're able to love other people around you. When you respect yourself, you respect those around you the same way. If you're honest with yourself, you're honest to everybody else in the same way. If you're

The Ojibwe, the third largest Native American group in the United States, are also known as the Ojibway and the Ojibwa. In the United States they are most often referred to as the Chippewa. The words are close—if you add an "O" to Chippewa, O-Chippewa easily becomes Ojibwa. The word "Ojibwe" is related to the Algonquian word "puckered" which is believed to come from the style of their puckered moccasins. There are nearly 150 bands of the Ojibwe living today in Ontario, Manitoba and Saskatchewan in Canada, and in Minnesota, Wisconsin and Michigan in the U.S.

In the Ojibwe language, a chief is called a "Gimaa" or "Ogimaa." In the past, chiefs were chosen by the band council, and were usually a son, son-in-law or nephew of the previous chief. But the Ojibwe traditions have evolved with the times. Today, men or women can be Ojibwe chiefs, and chiefs are elected through a democratic voting process.

going for your dreams, reach for them, don't let anything get in the way and always keep in mind that people will try to cut you down."

Frank recalled one occasion when he was speaking to a group of younger people. He was discussing how others would try to stop you from succeeding. He had just said, "People will cut you down," when a woman walked into the room. Frank recalls, "Just as I said it, an elderly woman came in and started cutting me down. I thanked her. If I believed the things she was telling me, I wouldn't feel good about myself."

Frank Abraham lives within his Ojibwe community with his wife, Rhonda. They have eleven children.

Senator Ben Nighthorse Campbell

UNITED STATES SENATOR

On April 13, 1933 in Auburn, California, the future United States Senator Benjamin Nighthorse Campbell was born. His Cheyenne name, Sunka Wakan Ahape, translates in to English as "Horse Goes at Night." or "Nighthorse." The name Nighthorse is a source of pride for Ben Nighthorse Campbell, even though his family history is wrought with tragedy and heartbreak. The road that he and his ancestors have had to travel was not an easy one.

When she was just a child, Ben's grandmother was kidnapped and taken from her home by a gang of "comancheros"—renegade traders from New Mexico who dealt in alcohol, guns, and kidnapped Indian children. They sold Ben's grandmother to a wealthy Hispanic family. She had to serve the family and do cooking, cleaning, and other household chores.

According to Ben, when his grandmother grew older she was considered very beautiful

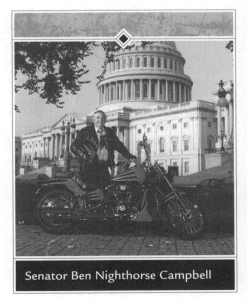

Senator Ben Nighthorse Campbell

by many interested male suitors. The story goes that she got into the middle of a fight between two men and was shot to death. Her orphaned son, Albert—Ben's father—was sent to a reservation in Montana with his grandmother. There he attended a Crow boarding school. Ben says about his father, "I can imagine it must have been pretty darn tough being a Cheyenne in an all-Crow boarding school in 1915. He probably got beat up six times a day by Crow kids."

When he was an adult, and after he had moved to California, Ben's father began to drink heavily. He drank himself to sickness and was admitted to a hospital recovery unit in California. Here he met Ben's mother, Mary. She was in the hospital being treated for tuberculosis, which she suffered from throughout her life. Albert and Mary married a short time later. Ben says, "My mother had tuberculosis. She was in the hospital for twenty-six years. [My father] didn't go back to the Rez (Reservation). He just stayed there in the hospital where she was."

Ben grew up in the 1930s and '40s. These were difficult times for Native Americans, as Ben remembers all too well. He recalls how complicated it was: "A lot of [Native American] people who came to the cities in the 1930s and '40s would hide their identities. If they could, they would try to 'pass'—the word pass was used in the African-American community as well as the Indian community. It meant you could 'pass' for an Italian or dark-skinned Frenchman. There wasn't as much bigotry [against Italian or French people] as there was against the Indians or African-Americans. So, Mr. Blackhorse became Mr. Black or Mr. Greentree might become Mr. Green. They would change their names and they would hide their identities, [they changed] anything to do with Indians because they thought there would be less prejudice."

Though it felt difficult and shameful to hide one's own identity, it was often the safest thing to do. Ben remembers one experience very well. His father and three friends had gone out for a night of drinking. Later, the three friends dropped off Ben's father at their home and drove off. The three men were found the next morning. They had all been murdered. Ben remembers his own fear and his father's response. "I remember that after that, boy—[my father] really shielded [me and my sister]. He wouldn't let us around Indians at all. He was so afraid of what might happen to us. It was one of those things we grew up with in the '30s and '40s."

With a father who drank heavily and a mother who was suffering from tuberculosis, Ben and his sister were sent to live in orphanages. He would not see his sister for years at a time. Sometimes his mother would be well enough to visit them. But then she would have a relapse and have to return to the hospital. As Ben grew up, he often took to the streets. He neglected his schoolwork and eventually dropped out of high school and joined the U.S. Air Force. He was in Korea during the Korean War, and returned to the United States in 1951.

As Ben got older, he got wiser and eventually decided to change his ways. He recalls, "I realized education was pretty important, so I went to night school and did whatever I could to get my grades up so I could transfer to college." Ben succeeded and went to San Jose State College. With more hard work, he obtained his degree in physical education and fine arts, as well as his credentials to become a teacher.

Ben also found time to express himself through art. He had learned to make jewelry from his father. "When my dad was young he had Navajo friends and he learned [jewelry-making] from them. I used to watch him. We didn't get any money from it. We were poor so we used to trade it for food." Ben has thought a lot about how he learned to be an artist. He says, "I learned from [my father], but I also learned that, as you go on, if you have any artistic ability it comes to you by some sort of creative force. It's not like the things you learn in school. You can learn the mechanics, but the feeling, the design of it all, just has to come to you. I don't think it's something you can put into a can, into a book or on a tape. I believe there is a seed put into you by the creator. That seed, you have to explore and expand. Find the one he put there and work on that one. Don't do something you weren't meant to do. It came naturally to me to be a jeweler. If you were meant to be a lumberjack, stay off the dance floor. And if you were meant to be a dancer, don't go cut down trees."

In addition to jewelry making, Ben Campbell was also a talented athlete. He had trained and competed in judo for many years. In 1960, the Olympic Games included judo for the first time, and Ben was good enough that he was hopeful about competing at the 1964 Games. He won a spot on the U.S. Olympic team, and recalls the process from there. "I was on the Olympic team, but I knew I had to get stronger. In order to get better in sports, you have to go where the tough guys are. If you want to be the best, you don't hide out with the little guys. I went to Japan. I cashed in my life insurance policy so I could buy a plane ticket to Tokyo."

In Tokyo, Ben attended Meiji University as a "kenshu-sei," or a special research student. He studied Japanese culture and trained in their sports program. He lived off campus in a small apartment close to where some Sumo wrestlers trained. "We students were so poor, these Sumo guys took a liking to us and would tell us to come over and eat. They cooked a big community pot, a Sumo stew."

He also lived near a Japanese sword maker. He would often visit, and learned many techniques that he would later apply to his jewelry making. "Japanese sword making has been handed down century after century. It's done in families. You just don't go and learn it. You inherit this way of learning from your ancestors in Japan. Some things they will let you watch and some things they won't teach you. It's not prejudice against being American, you have to be family. One of these things is the temperature of the oil or water that you temper the metal in. Nobody knows that except the master."

Ben gained techniques that would greatly improve his skills as a jewelry maker, and at the same time he developed his skills in judo. He began his training as an underclassmen or "Kojai." He washed the upperclassmen's uniforms and cleaned toilets. His actual judo training was even tougher. If an opponent was knocked down, the winner kicked him in the face or stomach. "It was nothing personal," Ben recalls. "You lose a match, you shave your head. It was an act of humility. They followed 'bushido'—the warrior way. That temperament is transferable. You learn it in sport, but you can transfer it to business, to politics, to anything."

Judo training was extremely tough. Ben's nose was broken nine times and he had to have his ears drained of fluid to avoid "cauliflower ears"—permanently swollen ears. But through this challenging training, Ben's skills dramatically improved.

Throughout his schooling, Ben never forgot about his American judo teammates. He continued to compete with them, and during his training in Japan, Ben would travel to compete with his American team in different countries. By the time he represented the United States in the 1964 Olympics in Tokyo (he was the team captain), Ben had already won the U.S. Judo Championship three times. He had also won a gold medal at the Pan American Games in 1963, in São Paulo, Brazil.

Ben's time in Japan was not only spent training. He also worked as a teacher of English, and he was an actor in Japanese movies. He laughs, "It was stuff you wouldn't watch but it paid well. One time I died three times in the same movie. I was a Russian soldier, an American soldier and a French soldier. It was called "The Last World War" or something like that."

After four years in Japan, Ben returned to the United States. Once again he experienced culture shock. Ben thought that American-style judo training was not good enough and so he started his own judo classes. As a teacher and coach, he did not hold back. In the middle of winter, his students trained without heat and with the windows wide open. "I pushed them the same way I had been trained in Japan. Boy, we won everything in sight for years. Three of the four [judo competitors] that went to the 1972 Olympics were my kids."

The strict training schedule—five hours a day, six days a week became too much and Ben eventually moved on. He began to teach school and worked nights as a sheriff's deputy. He also became a counselor to Native American convicts at Folsom Prison, near Sacramento, California. One day, Ben left the prison and stopped at a small trading post. "I walked in, and I'll be darned if I didn't see a necklace that I had made years before. I said to the lady, 'Where did you get that thing? I made that when I was a youngster!'" The woman had found the necklace. She asked Ben to make her another piece of jewelry. He says, "I went home and got out some of my Dad's old tools. When I took this necklace up to her, she said, 'That's great, I'll give you four hundred dollars.' I said, 'Four hundred dollars! You're going to give me four hundred dollars for that? I'm going to make you another one!'"

That woman talked Ben into entering his jewelry into the Gallup Intertribal Trade Show. His rings won first, second, third and "best of rings" in the show. Ben continued to enter shows and won more than two hundred ribbons. In one year alone, he won the Gallup Intertribal, the Santa Fe Indian Market, and the California State Fair. In 1972, Arizona Highways, a popular magazine, did a series on Indian art. They featured Ben Campbell in an article entitled "The New Indian" which focused on Native people who were experimenting with techniques and unusual materials. Nearly twenty pieces of Ben's jewelry were featured, and he gained the recognition he deserved for his art. As a result, he was able to make his living doing what he loved.

It was around this time that Ben met his wife, Linda, and they moved to Colorado. Ben's success in jewelry making continued and the demand for his work grew. He even used a small plane to make deliveries. One night in 1982, a bad storm prevented him from making a delivery to California. This resulted in a coincidence that would eventually lead him into politics. "I picked up a paper and read that there was a political meeting in downtown Durango (Colorado). I thought, I've never been to one of those, maybe I should go down and see what they do."

At that meeting, Ben ran into an old college friend who was running for sheriff. Ben offered to speak on his behalf and his friend won the nomination. They were also taking nominations for Colorado State Legislator. Whoever was nominated would have to run against a formidable and qualified opponent. Ben remembers, "They asked one guy if he'd run and he said he didn't have the time. They asked another guy and he said, 'Geez, I'm too busy.' I was on the end of the bench, and they worked their way down. They said, 'Will you run?' I asked, 'Well, what do you do?'

Ben Nighthorse Campbell lives on the Ute Reservation in Colorado with his wife. He continues to make jewelry, and is a Senior Policy advisor to the U.S. Senate.

'Oh, we'll show you,' they said. 'Does it take much time?' 'No.' 'Does it cost much money?' 'No.' so I ran for the Colorado Legislature 59th District. The other guy would have been a fine elected official. I just out-worked him. I walked to every house and went to every door. It was the judo training mentality. You just don't give up. So I won. I did two terms."

After four years as State Legislator, Ben decided to leave politics. But then he was given an opportunity to try politics again in 1987, when he was asked to run for the United States Congress. Only five incumbents—people who were previously in office—lost that year, and one of them lost to Ben Nighthorse Campbell. He ran successfully for three terms and then, in 1992, a Senate seat opened up. Ben was being offered an amazing opportunity. "I was only going to do one more term in the House of Representatives. I didn't want to be a lifetime politician. But a friend asked if I would give it a try. I won the open Senate seat."

As an advocate for Native American rights, newly elected Senator Ben Nighthorse Campbell was in the perfect position to truly help tribal peoples across the country. "I did some good at getting bills passed for Indian country. [But then] I got really upset with the Democrats—not individually, because I thought there were some pretty good people. But I thought the party leadership was going too far to the left."

In 1995, Ben changed his party affiliation from the Democrats to the Republicans. Some people feared this move would work against Native Americans, but Ben's reasons were thought out and it actually proved to be advantageous to the Indian people. "It was probably the best thing I could have done for Indian country," Ben recalls. "Most Indians are in the Democratic Party. Most of them vote Democrat. But the majority party controls the chairmanships."

As a Republican, Ben was working with the party that was able to pass the most legislation. As part of the majority, Ben had more power to put toward the Indian effort. "I got a lot of legislation passed—nearly thirty-two bills: Land Consolidation, Education, Strength in Tribal Courts, Water, you name it. A lot of Indian components were attached to the bills." When an Indian component was attached to a bill, reservations received a percentage of state funding that was related to that bill. If the state received funding for highways, for example, the component attached to that bill ensured the state's reservations would receive funds as well. Before this, Ben say, "States would spend the money how they saw fit and not include the tribes. States rarely helped the tribes do anything. The same applies to energy or anything else. If there is not an Indian section, they just get totally left out. They were left out in Homeland Security. I think that's where I did the most good—attaching bills to other bills that had an Indian component. We passed a lot of self-standing bills too. The Museum of the American Indian, for example—they opened it a month before I left. After all these years, it's just a delight to see it open its doors."

On January 3, 2005 Ben retired from the United States Senate. His career in the Senate was a great success. Many tribal chiefs and tribal members continue to thank and praise Ben's work today. "They do all the time," he says. "[But] the downside is that they got to relying on me an awful lot. The way Senate rules work is that any Senator can stop a bad bill by filibustering it or putting a hold on it. It got so all they had to do was come to talk to me and I'd fix it for them. A lot of them still tell me, 'we didn't know how lucky we had it when you were there to protect us.' But you know, there's never a right time to leave. In a way it feels good, but there's also a guiltful part. I see things happening now that I know I could have easily stopped. Now I've got to go over there and lobby and get friends to stop it."

Ben Nighthorse Campbell has accomplished so much in his life. He was a judo champion, a teacher, a deputy, a Congressman and a Senator. Ben is also a Cheyenne Chief. He was inducted to fill one of forty-four seats as a lifetime chief in the Cheyenne tribe. He has been through the ceremonial process that allows him to wear a full headdress. In his headdress, each feather represents a good deed in his life. With all of the accomplishments and good deeds in Ben's life, the tails of his headdress are very long. He is also a Sundance Priest, as well as a member of the Gourd Dance Society.

In his spare hours, Ben likes to speak to children, both Native and non-Native. He loves to share the wisdom of his life's lessons. Ben says, "Believe that you're doing the right thing when you're doing it. You have to do that. Otherwise

Ben is also a Cheyenne Chief and has been through the ceremonial process that allows him to wear a full headdress. Each feather represents a good deed in his life.

you're always questioning yourself. When I was in Office, when I was making decisions, it wasn't always based on what was best for the party or what was best for someone else. I kept thinking, 'I have to look in the mirror.' It's difficult for Indian kids—they're caught between cultures. In a lot of places in America there is still a lot of bigotry towards these kids. They feel it, they hear names being called. I just tell them, 'you just have to focus on one thing and let the rest bounce off of you. You're not going to change them all. If you want respect, it doesn't come free. Do good work, do good deeds, do good things.' It's unfortunate that in human nature some people still believe the way to build themselves up is to tear somebody else down."

Ben encourages children to make change in the world by using peaceful tactics. "I've got a lot of friends who believe changes can be made in the social structure by toe-to-toe and jaw-to-jaw confrontation. Throw your body down at the Columbus Day Parade, that sort of stuff. Those types are rarely involved in food drives for underprivileged kids or trying to get heat in some Indian elder's home. I've always believed that if you want true societal change, [you should] do it the way Martin Luther King, Jr. did it. He took a lot of abuse when he was alive, but look at the changes he made nationwide. I believe Indians can learn from that lesson. You can make changes in society and win respect without getting confrontational and threatening to burn down the house. You can burn down the house, but that doesn't make them like you. It just makes them hate you more. You can throw your body down at a parade, but do you think that makes them like you? Nah, it makes them hate your guts. So then when you go back because you need some help to do something good for your community, they're not going to give you help. They see you as the enemy."

Ben also shares his thoughts regarding the future of the Indian community. "I talk to a lot of Indian youngsters. We still have a terrible dropout rate, a lot of problems with alcoholism, escapism and violence. But I know in my heart it's getting better." Ben's optimism comes from his hopeful encounters with Native youth. He says, "I meet more and more young Indian people that really have direction and really want to do something with their lives. That's encouraging. We have a long way to go but we've come a long way too. In some states there are still laws on the books against certain Indian practices. We had a lot further to go than everybody else. Every person in this country who came from somewhere else had nothing to lose and everything to gain. For the Indians it was the other way around. We had everything to lose. And we almost did [lose everything]. We had a lot farther to go than everyone else because we had to turn it around. I'm talking to more and more youngsters now. Used to be, 'I got to get off this Reservation, I got to get out of here and find a job and leave.' That's not happening now, Indian kids [now say], 'I want to go to college and become a doctor and I want to go back and help my people.' You see that more and more. That can only be good."

Ben Nighthorse Campbell should be proud of the significant contributions he has made. The world has become a better place due to the work and commitment of this courageous man. Today, Ben Nighthorse Campbell lives on the Ute Reservation in Colorado with his wife. He has two grown children. He continues to make jewelry, and is a Senior Policy advisor to the U.S. Senate.

Senator Ben Nighthorse Campbell was the second Native American to become elected to the Colorado Legislature. He was awarded Outstanding Legislator of 1984 by the Colorado Bankers Association. The Denver Post and News Center 4 conducted a poll and Ben was named one of the Ten Best Legislators of 1986. Senator Ben Nighthorse Campbell was the first Native American to serve in the U.S. Senate.

LITTLE BIGHORN BATTLEFIELD NATIONAL MONUMENT

The Cheyenne were a strong tribe and many Cheyenne warriors were present at the Battle of Little Bighorn in Montana, in 1876. Also known as Custer's Last Stand, this was one of the most significant battles between Native Americans and the U.S. Army. Lieutenant Colonel George Armstrong Custer and his Seventh Cavalry soldiers were defeated by the Indians in a bloody battle in which many lives—both white and Native—were taken. In 1991, Senator Campbell won the fight to change the name of the Custer Battlefield National Monument in Montana to "The Little Bighorn Battlefield National Monument." This legislation honors the American Indians who died in battle.

Chief Tom Porter

CHAPLAIN FOR THE NEW YORK STATE DEPARTMENT OF CORRECTIONAL SERVICES

Tom Porter comes from a long line of Mohawk fighters, leaders and healers, and he has used this legacy to improve the lives of Native people for many years. His commitment to education and to maintaining Mohawk traditions is inspirational, and we can all learn from his example.

Tom Porter was born near the Mohawk reservation in Rochester, New York in 1944. After Tom's birth, his family returned to their farm on the Mohawk reservation. Tom recalls, "We lived on a farm, and I remember there was no electricity. There were no telephones, not even an [electrical] pole on our reservation. Everyone had kerosene lights, no television, no refrigerators, nothing. I was ten years old when the first electric pole came to our land." Life was simple for Tom and his family, as it was for many Mohawk families at that time. When electricity was first introduced to the Mohawk community, there was

Tom Porter

some resistance to what was considered the ways of white culture. "I remember a lot of people didn't want it. It was many years before families would hook up to it. Some hooked up to it right away but the majority did not. The Catholic priest had a lot to do with [the electricity coming to the reservation]. He wanted it because he got some money out of it. That's what my grandfather said, but I don't know if it was true."

His father, Robert "Bob" Porter was an ironworker and a superintendent who oversaw many building and bridge constructions in the state of New York. Bob was a fighter who had won Golden Glove boxing titles in Seattle and Rochester, and a third title on an aircraft carrier as a representative of the army. Tom's mother, Josephine Chubb, was also an athlete who had held the title of the fastest Iroquois and fastest Six Nation's runner. Josephine was also a traveling softball player. As Tom recalls, "She never talked about [her running] much, but I did find a photo of her going through the [finish-line] strings."

Tom's relationship with his grandfather and other elders was strong, and he comes from a family of spiritual and tribal leaders and healers. "My grandmother was a medicine woman. She got herbs from the mountains and the woods to heal people. Most of the older people her age were like that—it was nothing special. Most everybody in those generations were [medicine people]—they all knew medicine, it was not unusual, and it was quite normal. I grew up in the last [generation] to see that. They were the last of the real Mohawk people."

Tom was a spirited youngster and his grandmother had to come to his rescue many times. "I had fallen twenty feet from a tree and hit my head on a stone. I passed out and my cousin carried me back. My grandmother washed my wounds and fixed them with medicine. Another time, one of my cousins had a bike. I stuck my foot into it and sliced my ankle to the bone. She used medicine herbs and leaves and bandaged it with that. It healed good."

When Tom was six years old, he was exposed to his family's leadership activities. He recalls, "When I was six, I started to get involved with other tribes. That was when the Hopi came from Arizona to our longhouse. That was the first time I saw another Indian."

The elders of the tribe had always believed that children should be taught by the family and other elder tribal members. When Americanized schooling was brought to the reservation, the Mohawk people didn't trust it. They tried to resist, but non-Indians created a new school called The Mohawk School. And at age seven, Tom was forced to go. "My grandmother didn't want me to go there. We belonged to the longhouse. My grandmother was a clan mother and my grandfather was a religious leader in the longhouse ceremonies. A number of my family members were traditional people, so they didn't trust Americans and they didn't trust Christians."

Tom's family was concerned about the kinds of things that Tom would learn in a white man's school. As Tom remembers, "Education was to colonize the Indians and make them into white people. That's why [my family] didn't like it and I didn't like it. Everything was American, and they denied anything relevant to the Indians." Tom found himself trying to learn in a school that prohibited anything to do with Indian culture, spirituality or even Indian language. "Only Mohawk kids went to this school, it was called The Mohawk School but nothing Mohawk was allowed there."

At school, Tom was harshly disciplined and even abused if he did not follow the school rules and policies forbidding Indian culture or language. "When they tried to make us mind, they pulled our hair or pulled our ears or hit us with a ruler. Sometimes we would talk in Mohawk and they would hit us with rulers and say, 'We told you not to talk Mohawk!'"

Tom hated the Mohawk School and dreaded every day he attended. Frustrated and angry, and maybe showing some of his father's boxing spirit, Tom fought back. He remembers that "a lot of people would do nothing, they would just listen. But I was one who always argued back. I was fighting with the teachers and the principal all the time. They pulled our hair and we'd kick if we could reach them. I hated school. There was nobody on this earth who hated and despised school more than I did. There was not a day in my life that I ever appreciated going to school, not once."

Young Tom's life was not easy. His mother and father were divorced, and as the oldest of five children, Tom was obliged to help his mother raise his other siblings. After school and on weekends, Tom would work for white farmers, preparing meals and performing household chores. He would also pick strawberries, cherries, and apples at the fruit farms near Niagara Falls.

In spite of his dislike for school, Tom managed to learn English and in time, began to use his knowledge to help his tribe. "I used to be an interpreter for my grandmother. She never learned how to speak English. I used to go to the store with her and I would read [food labels] for her. If she couldn't find something, I would speak English for her to the white people."

At age thirteen, Tom began interpreting between the chiefs at the longhouse and the visiting government officials. "I didn't intend to do it. It was by accident. My family was in the traditional government and I was exposed to that."

Tom remembers frequent interactions between the Mohawk people and government officials, "[There were] fights over the seaway, fights with taxation, they were trying to make us pay taxes for our land. Then they took the land and sea away, and they dumped all of the stuff from the dredging onto our land, and they flooded some islands and took [other] islands."

Another formative event for Tom occurred when he was eighteen and wanted to enlist in the U.S. army to fight in the Vietnam War. The Tribal leaders were outraged and instructed Tom to return his military uniform. Tom obeyed and found himself a fugitive, running from the army. Two years later the FBI arrested him. Tom and the Mohawk people fought his case in court, arguing that Tom's enlisting would prevent him from becoming a leader of the Mohawk people according to Mohawk Law. They eventually won. Tom recalls, "[There] was a lot of turmoil and fear and anxiety. [At first] I wanted to go [to Vietnam] but the leaders did not want me to. Because if you kill somebody in a war, then you can never be a leader in our nation. Once you kill somebody, once you have blood on your hands, you can never be a leader. This is not American law, this is Mohawk law. This law is more than two thousand years old."

These early experiences of Tom's—his early positive involvement with his family of spiritual and tribal leaders, his difficult experiences as a young man in the Mohawk School, and his army court experience—all served to encourage his interest in the traditional beliefs and laws of his people. "A lot of Native people don't know their own laws, because they were colonized to become white people. So our job was to decolonize them and turn back to the Mohawks."

Tom listened to the tribal elders talk about ways to help Indians return to their Native roots and beliefs and decided to offer his help. In the mid-1960s, together with other volunteers, he began a group to help spread this important message, not just to Mohawks, but also to as many tribes as possible. This was the beginning of the "The White Roots of Peace," an organization of Mohawk people who traveled from the Mohawk reservation to hundreds of other tribal reservations across the United States, over a period of almost twenty years. According to Tom, it was "one of the most effective groups in the last two hundred years in Indian America" in terms of how they reinforced the importance of the Native American belief system.

The new, positive message of the White Roots was received with excitement by many but they also faced some resistance. "Not all of the Indians wanted to be Indians," says Tom. "The priests and nuns and whoever taught them religion had called them 'backwards people.' Nobody had faith in themselves. We went around and said, 'don't believe that, it's a bunch of lies. The Creator, when he made us, did a good job, and he'd be proud of it.' We would recite parts of our tradition and explain to them that the white people, the missionaries, and the educational system have told all the Indians that our ways to believe, our God, our Creator and our ceremonies are all Pagan, hedonistic, and backwards. [We taught Native Americans] to uphold tradition—no alcohol, no drugs—and to value their ceremonies and embrace all that the Creator gave to us before there even was a white man. Because God gave it to us, that's what he wanted us to be."

Traveling to so many different tribes was exciting but not always easy. Tom recalls some of the more difficult moments for the White Roots of Peace mission. "We would run out of money. Sometimes we would dance and put on a show, then pass the blanket to get money for gas to get to the next place. They were rough times because we were poor."

The efforts of the White Roots of Peace continued into the 1980s. During this time Tom met and married Alice, a Choctaw woman, and they started a family. Through his work with White Roots he had become committed to preserving the original language of the Iroquois and Mohawk people. He says, "The Germans can jump into the melting pot. The Swedish can jump in the melting pot. The Czechoslovakians can jump in there. The Polish can jump in there, too. But if some day those different nationalities...all lose their language as they jump in the melting pot of America, if someday their grandchildren want to learn it, even if they have lost it, the Swedes can go back to Sweden, the Italians can go back to Italy, the Polish can go back to Poland, and they can regain their language that way. But where does the Mohawk go? There is nowhere in the world for other Iroquois to go if they...want again to speak their language."

In 1979, Tom and a group of supportive Mohawk parents, who were also concerned with the survival of their language, co-founded the Akwesasne Freedom School. The school is an independent elementary school with a curriculum entirely in Mohawk. In 1985, the school began a Mohawk language immersion program—the only program of its kind in the United States. Students could study academic subjects such as reading, writing, math, and science, as well as learn about the history and culture of the Mohawks. The Mohawk ceremonial cycle and their "Thanksgiving Address," which teaches gratitude to the earth and everything on it, form the basis of their curriculum. Tom taught a range of subjects at Akwesasne Freedom School and later at other schools including on the Tyendinaga Reserve near Belleville, Ontario and at Trent University in Peterborough, Ontario.

Tom became known as "Sakokwenionkwas" or "The One Who Wins" and continued to serve his people as Chief of the Bear Clan, as an interpreter and as a cultural consultant for the North American Indian College of Ontario. In 1983, Tom started Partridge House, a Native American drug and alcohol rehabilitation facility and was asked to serve as a Chief of the Mohawk Nation, a role in which he served for several years.

During this period Tom and Alice tried to raise their six children according to the tradition of the Haudenosaunee long-house. This was a clan tradition where several families (from seven to as many as twenty) lived together in a wooden building of around 350 feet (106 meters) in length. The clan was a democratic group led by a council that offered a strong sense of belonging and identity for its members. For Tom, however, maintaining a traditional way of life became increasingly more difficult due to the increasing pollution on the St. Lawrence Seaway. Sewage and toxic compounds from industries, together with the growing number of casinos, bingo halls and bars on the Akwesasne reserve were destroying the waterway.

Tom remembered his grandmother telling him of the prophecy that the Mohawks would return to the Mohawk valley they had been forced to leave during the French and English Wars of the 1750s. The prophecy said that, "some-

Mohawk Chief Tom Porter wears a head of antlers as a sign of status.

day, our grandchildren will come back to the valley we left. They will rebuild the fire, and the sacred smoke will rise again." Tom, inspired by the prophecy, began a campaign to raise funds to purchase lands in the Mohawk valley.

In 1993, Tom fulfilled the prophecy by returning to his ancestral homeland. Together with a small group of tradition-al Mohawks, Tom purchased 322 acres (130 hectares) of farmland on the north side of the Mohawk River. The farm is known as Kanatsiohareke, the Place of the Clean Pot, after a collection of stones that look like overturned scoured pots. The community works togeth-er on the farm raising cattle and horses, and growing fruit and vegetables including corn and sacred tobacco. They also provide workshops on native history and culture and have created a work exchange program, in which students from schools such as Cornell University, Sarah Lawrence College, and Virginia Polytechnic Institute perform commu-nity services at Kanatsiohareke in return for presentations on Native history and philosophy at night.

Traveling with the White Roots of Peace had given Tom some recognition as a spiritual leader, however, when the Mohawk Nation took the State of New York to court, Tom's reputation became a national one. The Mohawks were look-ing for proper acknowledgment of Native American religious rights. They argued that the state must hire a Native Amer-ican religious leader to offer spiritual services to Native American prison inmates. The Mohawk nation won the case, and Tom Porter, endorsed by the Seneca, Onondaga, and Mohawk tribes, was hired as the Native American chaplain for the State of New York. As chaplain for the State Department of Correctional Services, Tom continues today to share native spiritual practices with inmates in the seventy-two correctional facilities of the New York prison system.

Along with the important work he has done to improve and enhance educational opportunities for Native people, Tom Porter is also an author of the book *Clanology: Clan System of the Iroquois* and other books. He has done much to improve the spiritual lives of Native Americans in our nation. The world is a better place due to his contributions, and his message of the importance of native tradition will resonate in our hearts forever. Tom lives with his wife Alice in New York. They have six children and many grandchildren.

The Mohawk are the easternmost tribe of the Six Nations of Iroquois. The six tribes include the Seneca, Cayuga, Oneida, Onondaga, Tuscarora, and Mohawk. The Mohawks are called The Keepers of the Eastern Door. Their tribal territory is unique. It lies in two countries along the Hudson and Mohawk River Valleys in Canada and the State of New York.

Mohawk chiefs are different in appearance than the stereotypical looking chief with a full-feathered headdress. The Mohawk chief wears a head of antlers as a sign of status. But even though a man was given the title of chief, he was still not above the respect given to the women of the tribe. If a clan mother disapproved of a chief's leadership, she could de-horn him, stripping him of his title. This guaranteed respect and compassion among the Mohawk leaders, men and women alike.

Stanley Vollant

ASSISTANT PROFESSOR OF SURGERY, UNIVERSITY OF OTTAWA

More than one hundred years ago, it was prophesized by the Innu people of Eastern Canada that some day one of their own would become a physician who would take care of his people and do great things. Many generations later, an Innu infant was born. His name was Stanley Vollant. His great-grandmother, the last of the Shaman healers of the Innu, took her great-grandson away to an undisclosed location on multiple occasions before she died. Some speculate that she transferred her healing gifts to the child.

Dr. Stanley Vollant

Stanley Vollant has fulfilled the Innu prophecy by becoming his band's first doctor. Not only did he become a doctor, but also he is a full-fledged surgeon and he teaches other young Aboriginal doctors. He uses his skills to provide services that are needed by his people, both young and old. And he encourages more Native youths to go into the medical profession.

Stanley Vollant was born in 1965, in Quebec City. His mother Claire was nineteen years old and a single parent. Claire had been a victim of severe abuse, and though she dearly loved her son, she doubted her ability to properly care for him. She considered adopting Stanley out to a new family, yet she was fearful that he would be raised without ever knowing about his own family, his history, or the culture of the Innu people. She eventually convinced Stanley's grandparents—her mother and father—to raise him.

Stanley was adopted by his grandparents and quickly grew to regard Xavier and Mary Anna as his parents. The family names were not aboriginal because of restrictions imposed by the Catholic Church. Stanley remembers, "It was forbidden by the church to have Aboriginal names. We had to have Catholic names. Stanley comes from Stanislaus, who was a saint. It was not acceptable to have any names not related to the church." But as a member of the Innu band, Stanley had pet names that his family called him. They called him "Kakuss," which means "porcupine," and his birth mother called him "Melua Petish," which means "small beautiful person."

After being adopted by his grandparents, Stanley moved to the Innu's Betsamit community on the east side of the St. Lawrence River. It was a change of pace from Quebec City to a small Innu community of approximately one thousand people, but Stanley was young and adapted quickly. His family did not have a car and instead traveled by a dogsled pulled by five dogs. They also traveled via canoe; Stanley remembers, "We had a small canoe without a rudder for small rivers, and a big canoe with a rudder for the strong currents of the Betsamit River. Conversations always regarded the tides. The river was twenty-five kilometers [15.5 miles] wide. Some days we could not see the other side of the river."

Stanley began at an early age to learn the ways of his people. "I liked being in the bush with my grandfather and grandmother. I often think of their teachings. They were

Catholics, but they had principles beyond Catholicism. It was the spirituality of their culture: respect nature, everything is linked together. One day we are going to come back to the herd and to the water, so we have to respect it. If we don't respect nature, it's going to go against us because we are a part of nature. We are part of overall creation. If you cut a tree, you have to give praise to the Creator because it is a gift the Creator is giving you. You do not destroy your agreement. If you destroy your agreement, you are destroying yourself. They [my grandparents] gave me the sense that I belong to nature. I belong to this part of the world. I belong to this river, I belong to this land, and we call it Nittasseinan, which means 'our land'."

Stanley was fortunate to receive this wisdom from his grandparents. But he was also expected to learn the culture of the white people. At age five, he had to attend the local school where he was expected to learn French. "The teachers were mostly nuns at school. We were forbidden to speak our own language because it was 'savage.' Even if we were outside in the open air speaking our language, we were punished. I had a hard time because I did not speak French at all. At home I was speaking Innu, and I was frustrated because at times it was easier to speak Innu than French. But at home at least I was able to speak my language."

The nuns were not alone in their beliefs that the Innu language and people were savage. Stanley was deeply aware of this attitude and felt it in many aspects of his life. Even the TV shows he watched contributed to this experience. He remembers a particularly meaningful time. "When I was young I would watch movies on TV about cowboys and Indians. [The Innu] never wore feathers. I liked the cowboys because they killed the stupid people with the feathers. They were easy to kill and they were very bad. I wanted to be one of those guys with the hats. When I began to learn French, I started to understand that those other guys were me! I banished western movies. I was so mad that my nation was portrayed as bad and stupid."

When he was six years old, Stanley's birth mother brought him to Montreal in an attempt to reunite the family. Not wanting to leave the people he already considered his parents, Stanley reacted badly. "I didn't feel at home, I didn't speak French very well and I fought every day with people. Sometimes the police had to come find me. After three or four months, my mother gave up and sent me back to Betsamit.

Stanley was happiest with his grandparents in the Betsamit community. Even though he attended a strict school and was punished for any Aboriginal-related behavior, nothing could compare to the positive influence he received from the teachings of his grandparents. It determined who he is as a person and has helped him to remain close to his Innu culture and spirituality. He received much of his teachings when he accompanied his grandparents into the bush. Even though time in the bush meant hard work, Stanley remembers the great times at the end of the days with his grandparents. "By 7 p.m. we had to go back into the tents because there were too many mosquitoes. So we would lie down and my Granddad and Grandmom told me histories. I remember the smells of the branches over the tents. And the sounds—I can still hear the voice of my Granddad. They told me about our village, our culture, and the creation of our world. They would sing to me. In the bush, my Granddad was the most marvelous man in the world. I named my son with the same name he has, Xavier."

When Stanley's beloved grandfather returned from the bush, however, he would often turn to alcohol. And he would be drunk for days at a time. He was never violent with Stanley, but he was neglectful. The electricity would get cut off and he was verbally abusive to the family. Stanley considers his grandfather's role in his life: "I should do everything that my Granddad did well, but I should not do everything that my Granddad did poorly. Nobody is perfect, but he taught me to be proud of myself and to be proud of my culture. I have to thank him. Without him I would not be here today. He never went to school, but he was a very intelligent man."

At the age of twelve, Stanley had to leave his grandparents and go to Quebec City to continue his education. He lived with his aunt's husband's family. Things were difficult in school, and Stanley was subjected to a degree of racism that he had not yet encountered in his life. He did not speak French as well as his schoolmates, and this made him a direct target. He was called "little savage" and told that, "You are poor. You don't talk the same way." He was always made to sit at the back of his classrooms and his grades began to suffer. "One thing that made me mad was that people would say, 'Oh you're savages, and you're not intelligent, you cannot be as intelligent as us.' I told myself, 'I can prove to them that Aboriginal people can be as good as and maybe better than them'."

Rather than being discouraged, Stanley became determined and was motivated by the cruel taunts of others. At the same time, he discovered that one reason his studies were suffering was that he had poor eyesight and needed glasses! After a trip to the optometrist, he could see the blackboard and was able to follow along with the rest of the class.

By his second year, Stanley Vollant became one of the best students in school. At the end of high school, he was named class valedictorian. But that wasn't all; he had also been a successful sportsman. He was a long distance runner on the track team and an offensive captain on the football team. Not only had Stanley Vollant shown people that an Aboriginal person could be the smartest person in school, but he could be a successful athlete as well. He had truly made an impression and was a source of pride for his people.

But even after high school, the career of this future doctor had not yet emerged. Stanley first considered archeology, but in the end did not find it to be exciting. The thought of building bridges and other structures interested Stanley, so next he decided to pursue engineering. He began undergraduate studies, but to his dismay he had to take time off when his grandfather had a heart attack. After his grandfather's recovery, Stanley returned to school and continued his studies. But then an even greater tragedy struck. A drunk driver killed his grandfather. He had been leaving a bar after a night of drinking and was hit by a car as he was walking down the road. A non-Aboriginal driver who did not suffer any consequences for his actions struck him. Even though people had seen the incident, the driver asserted that there was no proof he was behind the wheel. A jury found him not guilty.

Stanley was devastated; he felt justice had not been served in the case. The interruptions to Stanley's life and his studies had caused him to rethink his plans. A friend mentioned the possibility of Stanley going to medical school. He considered the option but there was a hitch, he had a horrible fear of blood and was terrified of dead bodies! He recalls, "I had a major problem about going into medicine because I had two fears. One was the fear of blood. Every time I'd seen blood, I fainted. And the second fear was of dead people. I'd always been a little bit scared of dead people. Maybe it was from the stories of my childhood."

Stanley liked the idea of medicine but dreaded the possibility of having to face his worst fears. But fate would take a hand, and Stanley would soon receive a message as to the path he should take. During a birthday celebration with his friends, Stanley happened across the path of an aboriginal elder that was known to have a serious drinking problem. Stanley had not decided what career path to take when the man insisted on speaking with him. "He stopped me and told me, 'I have to talk to you. I have just learned you are going to medical school next year. I am so proud of you. You are going to be the first Innu to become a physician. You will be able to treat elders who speak Innu only. You are going to be a pioneer in medicine.' Stanley insisted on leaving the man to join his friends, but the statements left a strong impression on Stanley.

Obviously the man had made a mistake. Stanley had not decided to study medicine. But the elder's words wouldn't leave Stanley's mind. He had made some convincing arguments, and Stanley thought that it might be true that he could make an important contribution to his people. He decided to give medicine a try. "It was so obvious. I wanted to be a physician because all that I wanted all my life was to come back to my village to help my people."

The next fall semester, he changed his studies from engineering to pre-medicine. His grades began to improve, and by the time he had completed his courses he had achieved an eighty-eight percent overall. He needed a ninety percent to apply for medical school, but with a letter of support from his band chief and the openness of the Assistant Dean at the University of Montreal, Stanley Vollant was accepted to medical school in 1984. The Innu prophecy was beginning to take shape.

Stanley entered his first year of medical school confident and ready to learn. He approached his subjects eagerly and was bravely ready to face his worst fears. But when his anatomy instructor told the class to meet the following day at the dissection lab to study the anatomy of the hand, Stanley grew apprehensive. "I left the classroom and went to my apartment. I was wondering if I was going to go back to medical school. I didn't sleep well. The next day we went to the anatomy lab, and people began to uncover the cadavers. I became a bit anxious. Then I told myself, 'it's a dead person. It won't move.' And then I fainted. I just fell down to the floor. I knocked my head. People were talking around me, and someone said: 'Oh, this guy won't be able to finish medical school if he fainted the first time.' The teacher asked me, 'Do you want to leave the class for a moment?' I told him no. After that I never had fear again about those bodies."

Stanley made it through his first year of medical school after conquering his horrible fear of dead bodies. He not only succeeded but also was leader of his class. But he had still to address his anxieties about the sight of blood.

In the second year of medical school, Stanley was slotted for clinical rotation with nine other medical students. The students would pair off for a few weeks and spend time in departments such as Emergency, Pediatrics, and Gynecology. Stanley hoped for a department that didn't involve blood. Psychiatry perhaps. But his first rotation was, of all things, Surgery. "I was scared and not very happy about what was happening. I went out on my bicycle and asked myself if I should go back [to school], because I knew I could not go back to the Operating Room. But I decided to go back."

When he returned to the school, a doctor asked Stanly if he would like to assist him with a surgery. Stanley decided that it was time to give it a try. He recalls, "When he started to do the cutting and I started to see the blood and the fat tissue, I turned green and blue and I don't know what color. And then I fainted. The nurses set a chair just behind me so I didn't fall on the floor. They asked if I wanted to come back tomorrow, I said 'No, I'm going to be able to do the rest of the surgery [now].' After that, nothing. I overcame my fear of blood. I didn't ever have problems after that." So after all his apprehension, Stanley was able to continue with his studies. He did the one thing that removes fears—he faced them head on. And amazingly, soon after he confronted them, they were gone. He was able to move forward with renewed strength, and nothing could get in his way.

Stanley continued to work toward his degree. In 1989, he graduated from medical school and fulfilled the prophecy of the Innu people by becoming their first physician. "I was very proud. I think people from my village were also very proud. They thought, 'Well, now there is no limit to being an Aboriginal person'." But the band's pride in their new doctor would only grow. Dr. Stanley Vollant wanted to pursue his education further and continue his medical studies. He would specialize in general surgery for an additional five years.

Stanley entered the world of surgery at an opportune time. Technology was making its way into the field, and old techniques were being abandoned to make way for new and improved methods. He learned techniques that improved recovery times and caused less scarring for patients. Laparoscopic surgery—also known as "minimally invasive surgery" or "keyhole surgery"—became Dr. Vollant's specialty. This highly technical surgery, in which the doctor operates on the abdomen with a telescopic lens through tiny incisions, is used mostly to remove a gall bladder or for procedures involving the colon. "It's like Nintendo," Stanley says. "You have to have synchronicity between your hand and your eyes. People recover very fast."

In 1990, Dr. Stanley Vollant would once again directly face racist assumptions and challenges. The Aboriginal world was thrown into turmoil through the infamous Oka Crisis. The Kanesatake Mohawk people of the Oka reserve in Quebec took action when the government and private contractors started to build a golf course on land the Mohawks believed belonged to them. Mohawk warriors created a blockade on the bridge between Kanesatake and Montreal, stopping traffic and people from moving across the river. Media coverage of the often-violent controversy was widespread, and during this period—between July and September 1990—Stanley Vollant would experience some of the worst racism of his life. "People didn't know about Aboriginals. In 1990, I think there was a waking up. But to everybody, we were all Mohawk. And there are fifty-five nations across Canada. I had to explain to everyone, 'I'm not a Mohawk. I am an Innu'."

Explaining to everyone about his heritage became a daily event for Stanley. His studying was challenging enough, but this new conflict was the cause of much frustration and anxiety. "The longer the crisis lasted, the more I became a radical. I became very engaged politically. I had to explain every day to the same people, again and again, about what

Aboriginal people want and about Aboriginal culture. It was quite frustrating."

The day came in the Oka Crisis when the Canadian Army was going to advance on the Mohawk people. Stanley feared there would be a massacre. He had made up his mind that if there was a massacre, he would leave Canada and continue his studies in Europe. Fortunately, there was no massacre and the crisis finally ended. Stanley Vollant stayed in Canada but he remembers well the effects of the crisis and speaks of it in retrospect. "It was the five months of my life that I find the most difficult. At the end of July, the Kanesatake Elders had to leave the town (of the Oka Reserve) because they were sick and needed medical care. As they crossed the bridge to Montreal, people from Montreal threw rocks at them. I was so upset to see those people throwing rocks at the elders. They were sick and people threw rocks at them because they were Mohawks. That I will never forget. I think we should educate non-Aboriginal people to the Aboriginal culture. I think there is a way that both of us—Aboriginal and non-Aboriginal people—can live together and grow up. If we know each other better, we can do great things. If we decide to stay away from each side and not try to understand each other, there are going to be fights forever."

In 1994, Dr. Stanley Vollant had completed his studies and he became a full-fledged surgeon. He moved to Baie-Comeau, a town near his home village, where he practiced medicine. For the first time in many years he was back close to his village and his people. Innu elders were overjoyed that for the first time a physician could speak to them in their own language. "I helped one elder who had esophageal cancer survive for three years. It is quite a long survival for a very advanced cancer. He said to me, 'that you became a physician is not an accident. It was written. It was destiny'." It was only then that Stanley learned of the prophecy, and he also learned that his great-grandmother was one of the last Innu shamans to have performed amazing healings.

Today Dr. Stanley Vollant lives with his wife and children in Ottawa. He travels frequently to the Betsamit community with his family.

In one incident, a youth had fallen from a tree and she performed a type of surgery to remove a blood clot through an opening in his head.

Stanley was overwhelmed. He found it hard to believe that he was a "chosen person." But his teachings as an Innu had never left him. Even though he had learned modern ways of healing, his Innu spirit shined through. "I didn't believe it at first, because of the way I was educated. But now, more and more, I believe maybe that's right. Maybe there is something we don't know. It can be from the spirits. The creator put me here on this earth to fulfill a destiny. My destiny is to be able to educate more Aboriginal people in medicine."

His desire to educate more Native people is already being met. He is the Assistant Professor of Surgery at the University of Ottawa. He is also the director of the Aboriginal Program at that University, which promotes medical education for Native people who are considering getting into the medical profession. His efforts have been recognized and he has gained great respect from his colleagues in the field. In 1996, the Governor General of Canada named him a Distinguished Aboriginal Role Model; from 2001 to 2003, he was President of the Quebec Medical Association; and in 2004 he was recipient of a National Aboriginal Achievement Awards.

Today Dr. Stanley Vollant lives with his wife and children in Ottawa. He travels frequently to the Betsamit community with his family. He tells his children the same histories and legends that were told to him by his grand-

Stanley Vollant's grandparents told him many traditional Innu stories. He remembers the Wendigo legend, in which people who were starving ate other people and became evil beings. And he recalls the story of the man in the moon. He remembers, "This man was not a good man and he did not want to share. The Creator sent him to the moon. He then had to share his light with the world every night. Every time I see the face, I remember my Granddad and Grandmom."

parents. To this day, Dr. Stanley Vollant feels overcome with emotion when he crosses the bridge to the land he knew so well as a child, and where he listened to the stories and songs of his grandparents.

Nearly one million Canadians are of Amerindian, Métis, or Inuit ancestry, but there are only about 160 Aboriginal doctors in Canada. Dr. Vollant suggests that there should be about 2,600. In 2005, the Association of Faculties of Medicine of Canada urged its members to promote the training of Aboriginal doctors. The University of Ottawa quickly responded by creating eight new spaces, and invited Dr. Vollant to head up their program. "The challenge of being able to provide medical training to young Aboriginals was a return to crucial, primordial and basic roots," he explains. The Faculty of Medicine hopes to train about one hundred new Aboriginal doctors by 2020. Dr. Vollant hopes that, through the program, non-Aboriginals will become more sensitized to Aboriginal culture in Canada. He would like medical students to take courses in the cultures, healing practices, and daily realities of Aboriginal peoples with an aim to developing a more respectful and effective cross-cultural approach to Aboriginal health care. "Specialists see you as 'a liver' or 'a breast.' For Aboriginal healers, it is important to consider the individual as a whole." They see health as a circle made up of four components: the mind, the body, the physical environment, and the social environment. The breakdown of any one of these leads to illness. In Dr. Vollant's view, this holistic approach to health could serve as inspiration for future physicians.

The Montagnais Innu live along the Betsamit River. According to French speakers, the river is known as the Betsiamite; to English speakers the river is the Bersimis. The Innu consider both names to be wrong and refer to it by its correct name, the Betsamit. But the Innu take the corruption of the name in stride, and perhaps even laugh about it. In fact the French even referred to the Innu as the "Papinachua"—the laughing people.

Laparoscopic surgery, which uses robot arms and miniature cameras, has some amazing benefits according, to Dr. Vollant. "Before, gallbladder surgery took about an hour and people stayed in the hospital for four or five days, and they could not go back to work for months. With laparoscopic surgery, it's a twenty-five-minute surgery. They come in the morning and go back home the same day. In ten days they can return to work. It's fantastic—the scar is just four small holes, instead of an incision about a foot long."

Raymond Cross

TRIBAL ATTORNEY

I t was May 20, 1948 and George Gillette, Chairman of the Fort Berthold Indian Tribal Council, covered his face with his hands and wept. He had just watched United States Secretary of the Interior Julius Krug sign a contract that enabled the U.S. government to purchase 155,000 acres of land from the Mandan, Hidatsa, and Arikara Indians of North Dakota. According to the contract, Indian land that had been deemed untouchable by previous U.S. treaties was being taken away to make way for the construction of a super structure known as the Garrison Dam.

The eventual creation of the Garrison Dam would cause flooding to more than 200,000 acres (81,000 hectares) of lush, fertile Native farmland. Out of more than 530 Mandan, Hidatsa, and Arikara homes along the Missouri River, nearly 450 fell into the flood zone. Prime agricultural land would be lost forever and entire generations of Native people would be forced to move to higher and less fertile land. In return, they received a small cash payment, a series of broken promises

Raymond Cross

(including promises for free hydroelectric power and medical facilities), and the loss of livelihood and community.

A few years after the Garrison Dam contracts were signed, six year-old Raymond Cross would watch his birthplace of Elbowoods, North Dakota vanish underneath the rising floodwaters of the Missouri river. Raymond experienced firsthand the devastation of the Mandan, Hidatsa, and Arikara people, and vowed that he would not let such damage to his people remain unanswered. One day, Raymond would leave his home in North Dakota and return as a "Coyote Warrior," a fearless tribal attorney who would go head-to-head with the U.S. Government in defense of his ancestors.

Raymond Cross was born "White Duck" on August 24, 1948, six years before the Great Flood. Raymond's father, Martin Cross was tribal chairman to the Mandan and Hidatsa. He married Dorothy Cross, a homesteader who had studied to be a nurse. Her skills as a nursing student were useful in a home of eleven children. Raymond was the youngest. He remembers that his upbringing after the flood was not easy. "It was an old-time upbringing, with chores like chopping wood and drawing water. We had to pour boiling water down the well sleeves, it took twenty or thirty minutes to prime them, and the wells were four hundred to five hundred feet deep. My mother cooked all the meals for seven to ten kids on a coal and wood stove."

Life had been easier in Elbowoods, the town where Raymond's family lived before the flood. Raymond remembers a little of the place that had provided a rich and fulfilling life for the Mandan, Hidatsa, and Arikara people. "We used to go down to the pasture to pick chokecherries; we grew our own food." The Mandan, Hidatsa, and Arikara had lived for generations along the Missouri River, and the community had flourished prior to 1954 and the damage wrought by the Garrison Dam. These strong, influential and self-sustaining people had been reduced to a community almost entirely dependent on government support.

The movement of the tribe to higher ground was a source of frustration, humiliation and great sadness. A division of the Army Corps of Engineers attempted to help before the actual flood, but many of the efforts of the military were unsympathetic. After leaving for only a few hours, one woman returned home to discover the Army had moved her house to a different location. Another couple was eating dinner when they heard a commotion. When they looked outside, Army engineers were in the process of lifting and moving their house.

Some people were not as fortunate as the others, and were unprepared when the flood moved in. Entire families scrambled to save personal belongings and valuables. At the last minute, athletic trophies from the high school were rescued by rowboat.

People were forced to move uphill to a town named Parshall. Raymond and his family did not fare well with the changes. Raymond's father had fought fiercely with Congress to stop the Garrison Dam, and when that battle failed in 1949, he spent another seven years fighting a losing battle for compensation. His grim experiences took their toll, and he turned to alcohol and sought divorce from Raymond's mother. Raymond recalls some of the damage: "Elbowoods was flooded. There were five communities up and down the Missouri Valley that were all flooded. They had to move to the high plains, a difficult, desolate, arid environment where it was hard to do anything, especially agriculture. After the flooding a lot of Indians moved into that periphery of the reservation. I grew up in a place called Dog Town—because of all the dogs in that town. That's where a lot of the homes were relocated to."

Raymond's older sister Phyllis remembers how hard those days were. She says, "It's still hard to talk about. We lost everything. Everything that told us who we were for thirty generations vanished. Raymond and Carol (his sister) grew up thinking it was normal to see the parents of their friends passed out drunk in the streets. Raymond never talks about those years. He walled it off. That's how he survived as a

Raymond Cross had an old-time upbringing, with chores like chopping wood and drawing water. His mother cooked all the meals for seven to ten kids on a coal and wood stove.

little kid. He could walk through a burning house and not know it was on fire."

Although life was difficult, Raymond continued to live his life as best he could. He decided early on to become the best person he could be. He turned his attention toward his studies in school.

After attending school for a number of years, he began to notice something peculiar about what he was being taught. "In middle school or junior high I was learning about our state of North Dakota. How we have six varieties of corn, about farm life. But what was lacking was any mention of Native Americans or any of the three affiliated tribes whose land we were on. What you begin to realize is that we're sort of in exile in our own land. We were completely written out of any story."

Raymond did not allow his exclusion from white society to hold him back. He continued to work diligently in school. When he was in high school, a relocation program was available for Native people in the Great Plains area. Young men and women were given one-way bus tickets to large cities such as Washington D.C., Chicago, or San Francisco. "My brothers and sisters took the option and were living in the Bay Area of San Francisco in the late fifties and early sixties. My sisters invited me to come to California and go to Santa Clara High School outside San Jose."

Raymond found life in California to be much different than in North Dakota. He was immediately struck with culture shock. "I went from a tiny school of thirty-five students to an open air giant school of three thousand students." He also met with segregation. "I was put into a class with all brown-skinned students, all the Hispanic students." He was introduced to the Mexican culture outside of school as well. When he was not in school, he would work alongside Mexican farm laborers in the fields.

Raymond continued to work hard at his studies, and his efforts were eventually recognized. His teacher asked if he would like to take more advanced classes. Raymond accepted the offer and found himself in a different world. "I moved into another class and it was all white kids. It was like night and day."

Raymond continued to meet the growing challenges in advanced studies classes. Upon graduation, he was offered a chance to go to Stanford University, with scholarship assistance from the Bureau of Indian Affairs (BIA). "People may criticize the BIA, but it was only through the administrative flexibility of the Aberdeen Area office [that was I able to go to Stanford]. They paid for my education, they looked at my scores and my record and said, 'Usually we don't do this, but based on what your counselors tell us, based on what you say in your essays, we're going to change our rules and let you do this.'" After graduation, Raymond found himself at prestigious Stanford University.

Raymond had always noticed that in the course of all his teachings, the Native American contribution to history was non-existent. Now that he was attending such a renowned institution such as Stanford, he felt empowered. He looked seriously at the possibility of turning to law as a profession. "People began to talk for the first time about the possibility of using law as a means to rectify some of the historic injustices. I have to say I got caught up in some of that."

Raymond decided to follow law and was accepted into Yale Law School. Although he had a degree from Stanford, Raymond still faced personal challenges. "I began to realize that a lot of these kids came from environments that were different than mine. [They had gone to] private boarding schools. I realized that these guys really knew their stuff. They had been groomed since private pre-school to accomplish their life plans."

But for Raymond, being intimidated was not a deterrent. He continued to persevere and graduated from Yale in 1973. Raymond then took the final step, and passed the Bar Exam to become a lawyer. He says, "The only choice I ever really made was to go into Indian Law." Some years later, he would earn the title "Coyote Warrior."

In 1973, Counselor Raymond Cross went to California and began working for the California Indian Legal Services (CILS) offices. After two years, he moved on to the Native American Rights Fund (NARF) based in Boulder, Colorado. It was through NARF that Raymond worked on his first big case, fighting for the Klamath Tribe in Oregon. The tribe had been terminated by Congress in the 1950s and had lost all of their rights to their water for sustenance and irrigation. Raymond Cross was successful in helping reinstate the Klamath as a federally recognized tribe and secured their rights to water in the Klamath Basin. The case set a precedent for other tribes to reclaim their water rights in other federal courtrooms across the country. Raymond's name was becoming very well known in federal courtrooms and Indian communities.

Even though Raymond lived in the Boulder, Colorado area for many years, he still felt drawn to his roots among the Mandan, Hidatsa, and Arikara people. In 1980, the tribe created its own legal department. Even though he would have to take a reduction in his income, Raymond did not hesitate when he had the opportunity to work for his own people and to pick up where his father had left off so many years earlier. "One of the things I've always wanted to do was to come back and work for my own tribes," he said. But at the onset, the tribal council was not completely receptive. "It's hard because your family connections are still alive, people feel you're trying to come back and reassert that family control. The vote to hire me was five to four."

He was not completely trusted at first by the tribal council, but Raymond would earn their confidence. His first opportunity came through his assignment to special projects, specifically a challenge to broken agreements of 1949 and an attempt to gain some retribution for the losses incurred because of the floods.

But this was no easy beast to conquer; Raymond had his work cut out for him. Years passed as he worked for justice for his tribes. Things were looking up and the possibility of obtaining retribution was beginning to look like a reality. In addition, the tribal council recognized Raymond's efforts as genuine. They saw his intentions were unselfish and when his contract came up for renewal, the vote was nine to zero in his favor.

Raymond's efforts continued with total support of his tribal council. As it turned out, the Mandan, Hidatsa, and Arikara people were not the only ones suffering from damages inflicted from the construction of the Garrison Dam. The dam was originally built on the premise that the dam would regulate the flow of the river to prevent future flooding in downstream states. And they had planned that large amounts of water would be available to nearby farmland via irrigation. After the dam was built, however, no irrigation system was ever created. In an effort to ease the frustration of the farmers and their neglected farmlands that were denied water, an investigative commission called the Garrison Diversion Unit Commission (GDUC) was created. The GDUC would provide the opportunity Raymond needed to right the wrongs that the U.S. Government had inflicted on his people.

The GDUC hearings were held in Fargo, North Dakota in October of 1984. The hearings would allow a long line of frustrated farmers to state their case against the Garrison Dam. The commission members listened to one complaint after another and would eventually present their findings to the government. The commission never considered that they would hear anything regarding Native American tribes.

For five days, Raymond Cross waited patiently to have his chance to speak. At the final moments, it appeared as though the commission would close the proceedings without giving Raymond a chance to speak. Literally, as the commission was adjourning for the final time, Raymond seized the moment and stepped up to the podium. As he began to speak on behalf of his tribal people, the gavel cracked down, closing the proceedings.

Raymond demanded the opportunity to tell the story of his people, and promised that he would not be leaving until he presented his case. The Commission was intrigued. They could have ignored Raymond's presence but they decided to honor his request. They recognized him as the attorney for the Three Affiliated Tribes of the Mandan, Hidatsa, and Arikara Nations. He was given fifteen minutes to present his case.

Raymond proposed that a special study area be created to examine the enormity of the promises broken by the U.S. government. He described in detail the damages and injustices committed and he presented all of the broken promises that had been made to the three affiliated tribes. Raymond's arguments were so effective, his presentation was so strong, and the atrocities so great, that the members of the Commission sat up and listened. He finished his statements and sat back while the Commission decided the fate of the Mandan, Hidatsa, and Arikara people.

His arguments hit the mark. The Commission decided that the tribes had suffered undue hardships, which were directly caused by the creation of the Garrison Dam and the resulting floods. The Commission recommended to Congress that the tribal issues as presented by Raymond Cross should be directly addressed. In turn, a new Joint Tribal Advisory Committee (JTAC) was created to specifically address the issues regarding the injustices against the Mandan, Hidatsa, and Arikara people. It was a giant step in the right direction.

The JTAC traveled to North Dakota, and the appointed members of the Committee listened to the stories of grief and hardship endured by the tribe's elders. The stories were emotional and devastating, so much so that the direct testimony of the elders was admitted as evidence. This was another major victory for Raymond, who had worked long hours to find the elders to testify on behalf on the tribes.

The JTAC was deemed a great success, yet the report that was produced and submitted to officials in Washington D.C. seemed to lose steam and get lost in the red tape of Washington bureaucracy. Raymond worked to keep the report alive with help from the Mandan, Hidatsa, and Arikara Tribal Chairman Ed Lone Fight. As they grew nervous about the future of the JTAC report, an odd stroke of luck would fall in their favor.

Ronald Reagan was the U.S. President at the time. He was visiting Russia and meeting with government officials. When the Russians asked him about U.S. government relations with Native Americans, he remarked that perhaps the Native American people should have been allowed to stay in their "primitive lifestyles." The comment enraged tribal officials and the Reagan Administration raced to make amends.

Ed Lone Fight was one of the tribal officials who had been asked to sit with Ronald Reagan. When Reagan asked Ed how his tribe was doing, Ed discussed the delay in responding to the JTAC report. Reagan recognized a way to make good and turned to Secretary Donald Hodel to inquire about the status of the report. New light was immediately shone on the report, and Raymond Cross and Ed Lone Fight doubled their efforts to seek just compensation for their people.

In 1992, after frequent trips to Washington D.C., Raymond Cross would finally see a joint committee of the House of Representatives and the U.S. Senate award the Mandan, Hidatsa, and Arikara people $149.2 million for the illegal taking of treaty protected lands in 1949. Raymond Cross, who had worked tirelessly for many years, had sought and won a victory of compensation for his people.

There was only one hitch. Where would the money come from? Raymond remembers, "$149 million! The big battle was not over liability—even the general accounting office agreed with that. The problem was where would the money come from? Getting money from Congress is one of the most frus-trating [exercises]." Raymond had to use every bit of creativity he had. He worked with a public interest lobbyist by the name of Lee Foley, a man with connections on Capitol Hill. Togeth-er they came up with a creative plan to secure the money.

Raymond and Lee Foley presented a proposal in which the profits generated from the Garrison Dam would be put into a special account and the interest generated would go directly to the Mandan, Hidatsa, and Arikara. In six years, they projected that the interest would reach $149.2 million.

Even with the brilliance of Raymond's plan, the Three Affiliated Tribes Just Compensation Act still needed to be approved. It was in grave danger of being vetoed by then-new President George Bush Sr.

Lee Foley and Raymond Cross had one last ace up their sleeves. Congressman George Miller had been working on a Bureau of Reclamation Reform Act, the by-product of the original Garrison Dam committee's findings. Foley and Cross arrived at his office and were immediately brought before Congressman Miller. The Reform Act was nearly guaranteed to pass because it was tied to important political connections. Lee Foley and Raymond Cross jumped into action. They asked the Congressman if he would attach the Compensation Act to the Reform Bill. Impressed with their proposal, Con-gressman Miller reached across his desk and shook the hand of Raymond Cross, expressing honor at such an opportunity.

The Bureau of Reclamation Reform Act was passed, and along with it, the compensation of $149.2 million was approved for the Mandan, Hidatsa, and Arikara tribes. Ray-mond Cross, after years of committed effort, had finally achieved what his ancestors had strived for. He was able to obtain compensation for the atrocities against his people.

Raymond Cross has moved on from his position as tribal attorney for the Mandan, Hidatsa and Arikara. He is a law professor at the University of Montana and works extensively with Indian tribes, Indian organizations, and federal agencies on issues of Indian education, tribal self-determination, and cultural and natural resource preservation. His experiences in dealing with the Garrison Dam compensation issues have told in a book entitled *Coyote Warrior: One Man, Three Tribes and the Trial That Forged A Nation.* He enjoys working with younger people and sends advice their way. "Realize that in the most desperate and dismal circumstances, with some help from others, a lot of things can be accomplished. If you have an interest, a passion or an unquenchable desire to excel—whether it's artistry, music or sports—that sort of conviction will carry you. Regardless of what's going to happen, come heck or high water, say to yourself, 'I'm going to choose to do something with the talents that I have.'"

Raymond speaks directly to the Native American students, who may find themselves facing numerous challenges. He says, "Native American students have a unique mission, a special opportunity linked to their heritage, to the integrity of the past and to the strength of the future. That is to decide that they're not going to drink alcohol, they're not going to do drugs, they're not going to fall into the common path, they're going to make [positive] choices. I think that is a difficult road to follow. It's a road that many Indian people are choosing, including people on my reservation. That's why I'm optimistic about the ability of my tribal people back home to recover from the effects of the Garrison Dam project."

What about the term "Coyote Warrior," which is given to Indian tribal lawyers? Raymond responds with a smile, "The Coyote is associated in all Great Plains and other Indian societies as a kind of trickster figure. If you want to think of lawyers as trickster figures, I guess that's one way of thinking about it."

But Raymond Cross transcends the term. He is not merely a trickster; he is a true Native man of courage.

The Mandan, Hidatsa, and Arikara once flourished as three independent tribes. Because of a smallpox epidemic in 1781, and again in 1837, the tribes were nearly lost. They chose to unite and become one people. They maintained their individual tribes' set of personal beliefs and rituals, but came together for economic and social survival. Today, the Mandan, Hidatsa, and Arikara Reservation lie on both sides of the Missouri River. The impressive tribal government office, situated four miles from New Town, North Dakota is an obvious indication that the tribal council is alive and well. The council makes decisions regarding the health and good of their people and institutes education and other programs to ensure their tribe's livelihood.

Historically, the Mandan, Hidatsa, and Arikara were a brave people who had provided refuge to notable historical figures such as American explorers Lewis and Clark, in the early 1800s. A Mandan, Hidatsa, and Arikara leader known to some as Big White and to others as Black Cat was the only leader to accompany Lewis and Clark back to Washington D.C. to meet with government officials.

Raymond Cross' grandfather, Chief Old Dog, was born in 1850, a year before the Mandan, Hidatsa, and Arikara tribes signed a treaty with the U.S. government that recognized their perpetual ownership of twelve million acres (4,850,000 hectares) between the Missouri and Yellowstone rivers. A revered warrior in battles against the Sioux, Old Dog assumed the mantle of leadership passed down from his legendary ancestors, the chiefs who had sheltered Lewis and Clark in the winter of 1805. And though Old Dog never learned a word of English, and respectfully declined an offer of citizenship from the Great White Fathers in Washington, his son Martin—Raymond's father—would play the saxophone and raise cattle, enlist in the Army in World War II, and become personally acquainted with five U.S. presidents.

Lieutenant Mark Bowman

POLICE OFFICER

Residents of Virginia Beach, Virginia, can sleep peacefully knowing that the courageous and well-trained police officer, Lieutenant Mark Bowman, is on the job. Lieutenant Bowman —"L-T" as he is called by some of his colleagues— is a law enforcement officer for the Virginia Beach Police Department and works out of Virginia Beach's Second Precinct, near the resort town's busy ocean-front. His thirty-year career in law-enforcement has been a varied one. He has worked as a sheriff, a patrol officer, a member of the Virginia Beach SWAT team, a detective, a patrol sergeant, and an instructor of leadership principles to other officers in leadership positions. Many times the students he has taught have outranked him.

Mark enjoys his current position as Lieutenant. Lieutenants are middle level managers in the precincts. "Our role," Mark says, "is to assume 'incident command' or to take control of a serious situation that involves more than one squad." He gives the examples of a hostage taking, a serious car or plane crash, and describes a recent incident with a "barricaded subject." He describes how "one person was in a home, and she refused to surrender. It was a woman who had threatened her neighbors with a gun. We wanted to arrest her, but we wanted to do it without any violence. There

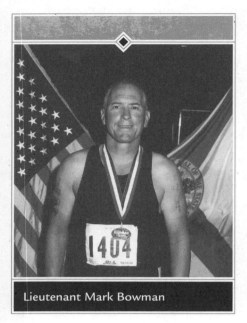

Lieutenant Mark Bowman

were multiple units involved. We had negotiators, patrol officers, and traffic officers. We had to establish a perimeter around the location. It took a couple of hours of negotiators talking to her to finally convince her to surrender."

Throughout his life and his long and varied career, Mark has always remained close to his heritage. He considers himself Choctaw, though his family lineage is a mixture of more than one Native American tribe. He explains his complex bloodline: "My mother is Canadian, my (paternal) grandfather is Choctaw, and my grandmother is Creek and Chickasaw. The tribes of the southeast were predominantly matrilineal, so one would trace one's family lineage through the mother's side of the family. As they became assimilated into American culture, they became more patrilineal. Legally we can only belong to one tribe. I belong to the Choctaw tribe because my father's father was Choctaw. But by blood, I'm more Creek and Chickasaw than Choctaw."

Despite, or perhaps because of, his varied heritage, Lieutenant Bowman is attentive to his culture. As well, members of his family have always contributed to his knowledge. His grandfather helped to keep their heritage alive through sharing various teachings with him. His father holds one of the peace pipes that were allegedly used at the signing of the Treaty of Dancing Rabbit Creek. Mark says, "I was always aware of my culture. My grandfather liked to talk a great deal about it. I am fortunate that a lot of information and knowledge was passed down through our family."

Other members of Lieutenant Bowman's ancestry were in the line of law enforcement. His great-grandfather was Deputy Marshal for Judge Parker in the western district of Arkansas in Fort Smith. Parker was infamously known as "the hanging judge." The Deputy Marshals at that time were predominantly Native American, and besides law enforcement their duties included collecting taxes. In 1896, Mark's great-grandfather wrote a letter in a pocket calendar in which he told the story of a shoot-out he was involved in. He mailed the pocket calendar to his wife to let her know that he had suffered a flesh wound, had arrested a man, and that he was okay.

Mark began his career as a sheriff in Little Rock, Arkansas in 1976. The standards and processes for becoming a police officer have changed a great deal since then. "It was a different time," he recalls. "They gave you a gun and a badge. I started in June [but] I didn't go to the Police Academy until October. I had no real training. You rode with someone, a more experienced officer. How experienced is another matter. He might have only been there six months longer than you. Early in your career it's all exciting because it's all new. It's exciting when you get to drive with your lights and sirens on. [It's exciting when] you arrest people. But then you also learn that a great deal of [the work] is mundane activities. Not that they aren't important, but they certainly couldn't be characterized as exciting."

After nine years with the sheriff's department in Little Rock, Mark moved to the Hampton Roads area of Virginia to be closer to his wife's family. In 1988, he began his career with the Virginia Beach Police Department. He began working as a patrol officer, and his interactions with the public would teach him many lessons.

One of the earliest lessons Mark learned was that some people viewed kindness as weakness, and that kindness in a police officer could be interpreted incorrectly by a criminal. But for Mark, it's important to be aware of the differences between right and wrong. "It's the right thing to do to be kind to people. Evil people don't see it that way. They see kindness as a form of weakness. You give someone a break because you want to be kind, you want to cut them some slack, and they take advantage of that. The next night you may find them doing the same thing. Why didn't this person learn this lesson last night? I cut them some slack in the hope that they would change their behavior. I quickly learned that they didn't view it that way. They viewed it as [I was] weak, and it excused or even facilitated their behavior."

Mark Bowman's traditional Choctaw wedding ceremony.

Mark remembers his interactions with one man who never seemed to learn a lesson, a Native American man he had arrested on multiple occasions. "I must have arrested him once a week," he says, and even though Mark wanted to help this man, he knew that he couldn't control the personal choices that the criminal made.

Mark had a job to do, and even when the situation isn't pleasant, police officers have to make the right decisions. Society may not always appreciate the actions of the officers, but it is important to recognize that because of them, our streets are much safer. And while some people may never change, there are many who change their lives for the better after being given a wake-up call by the justice system.

Mark Bowman continued his climb within the ranks of the Virginia Beach Police Department and was privileged to experience many aspects of the force. He was on the SWAT team, he was a detective, and he was a patrol sergeant who oversaw the work of the patrol officers.

Today, with his thirty-plus years of experience, Lieutenant Bowman has a unique and valuable perspective that many other law enforcement officers don't have. He has seen the techniques that work and the ones that fail. He knows what type of person can become a good police officer. When prospective candidates attend the police academy, the dropout rate is about thirty-three percent. He explains that it takes a certain personality to become a good police officer. "Most people who go into law enforcement—I don't want to say they've led a sheltered life, but they often haven't been exposed to a lot of things. We probably would [also] not hire [people] if they've been around a lot of crime in their lives."

Mark goes on to describe the difficult and often frightening revelations that are part of being an effective police officer. "The first reality check is when it really sinks in how evil some people can be. We all have a tendency to be a little selfish, [but] we've all been socialized to share, to think about other people and to be polite. In this profession, you start to encounter people who weren't socialized that way, and who will hurt other people just for their own gratification." The hardest part, Mark says, is "not so much the physical fear when you get into a fight or when someone wants to take your life. It's afterwards, that's the real gut check. There are people out there who are really different from me and from the rest of the world. You come to realize that one of [a police officer's] significant roles in society is to deal with those people, to cull them from the herd and send them to prison. I'm not a strong believer in rehabilitation—some of them have been in rehab several times. [To be effective] those activities have to be focused on a lot earlier in life. Not to say somebody can't change, but when they're adults and going to prison, [the ones who can be rehabilitated] are few and far between."

Since he first started in 1976, Lieutenant Bowman has seen major changes in the field of law enforcement. Technology has paved the way for improved methods of communication and response times. Computers used to be giant beasts that worked off punch cards in some dungeon-like room. Now patrol cars are outfitted with computers that allow officers to communicate with one another and to gain immediate access to criminal and Department of Motor Vehicle records. But with the improvements in law enforcement technology and communication methods, Lieutenant Bowman has found himself in an interesting dilemma. "The biggest problem I have is that there is more stuff on my belt now then when I started in 1976, but my waist hasn't gotten any bigger!"

Lieutenant Bowman describes with a smile the contents of an average police officer's belt pack. "We have a handgun and hot pepper (OC) spray. OC spray is a very effective tool that takes [the criminal] to the point where they can still breathe enough to survive, but not to fight. [We carry] an impact tool or collapsible tool; typically law enforcement officers in America have always carried a handgun and some sort of club. I have two ammunition clips and a set of handcuffs. I've had [the handcuffs] since 1981. These handcuffs are older than some of the police officers we have! One person has gone to death row in these handcuffs. We also carry a radio and a much better flashlight than the one we had available to us in 1976. When I first started, I carried only a nightstick, twelve bullets and a revolver."

Throughout his career as a law enforcement officer, Lieutenant Mark Bowman has never stopped trying to improve himself as a person. Education is very important to him, and he has received a Bachelor's degree in Criminal Justice and a Master's degree in Public Safety Leadership. And if that isn't enough, he is continuing his formal education. He recently completed the course work at Old Dominion University toward his Ph.D. Upon completion of his dissertation, Lieutenant Mark Bowman will be able to change his title to "Doctor Mark Bowman." Mark believes strongly in the value of formal learning. He says, "For young people, the one thing I would emphasize more than anything else is formal education. It's something we may not recognize, but when you think about the histories of our people, they had to be effective learners to survive. Formal education is just one method of learning—our people learned in the past through doing and through the school of hard knocks, which is also a very important kind of learning. But we're in a modern world and one challenge for many minorities is the view that knowledge is something that only the white man has. But how can anyone own that which you cannot touch? Knowledge is universal. No one owns it."

Lieutenant Bowman is a man who has put his life on the line countless times in his career. He has served in the front lines as a law enforcement officer and still pursued his education, learning on the job while also achieving multiple degrees. But was that enough? Not for Mark Bowman. He is also an established triathlon athlete who has competed in two Iron Man competitions. He has maintained an excellent physical

Lieutenant Bowman an established triathlon athlete who has competed in two Iron Man competitions.

appearance, not only through a simple, healthy diet and regular exercise, but also through a training regimen that has enabled him to compete in a race that includes a 2.4-mile swim, a 102-mile bike ride and a 26.2-mile marathon. Physical health is another important issue for Mark. He explains, "Fitness is another issue that Native people need to take more seriously. When you think about our past,

Before the arrival of colonists in 1607, the Natives who lived in today's Hampton Roads area were known as the Chesepians. "Chesepioc" is an Algonquian word that means "Great Shellfish Bay"—a reference to the bounty of Chesapeake Bay. Many Native artifacts, such as arrowheads, pottery, axes, and beads, have been found in Great Neck Point.

remember that we had to be fit in order to survive. You were fit or you didn't make it."

Lieutenant Bowman is due to retire in April of 2009 after thirty-plus years in the law enforcement profession. Although work has been important and a source of pride for Mark, he has always made it a point to separate his career from his private life. "I'm pretty resilient. It's an important profession, but it's not a crusade. When I retire in a few years, there is still going to be crime in Virginia Beach. I'm going to do the best I can while I'm here to deal with that. It's kind of like the saying, 'none of us are going to get out of this life alive.' You've got to recognize that [your work] is a piece of your life. You've got to have other pieces in your life. You have to stay fit. You have to spend time with your family. You have to do other things you enjoy. Your entire focus for your life can't be your profession."

After retirement, Lieutenant Mark Bowman will begin his next career as a college professor. He looks forward to having his summers and holidays off.

Golden Eagles Hotshots
> *All photographs courtesy Vincent Schilling*
> *Cover photo courtesy Vincent Schilling*

Patrick Brazeau
1. *Photo courtesy "Patrick Brazeau Collection"*
2. *Photo credit Deb Ransom, Office of the Prime Minister*
3. *Photo courtesy "Patrick Brazeau Collection"*
4. *Cover courtesy "Patrick Brazeau Collection"*

Red Hawk
> *All photographs courtesy Red Hawk*
> *Cover photo courtesy Red Hawk*

Larry Merculieff
> *All photographs courtesy Larry Merculieff*

Frank Abraham
> *All photographs courtesy Frank Abraham*

Senator Ben Nighthorse Campbell
1. *Photo credit Senate Photographer, George Dalton Tolbert IV*
2. *Photo courtesy Roni Sylvester*
3. *Photo courtesy Campbell family*
4. *Cover photo credit pending*

Tom Porter
> *All photographs courtesy Tom Porter*

Stanley Vollant
1. *All photographs courtesty Vollant family*

Raymond Cross
1. *Photo credit Todd Goodrich*
2. *Photo courtesy Cross family*

Lieutenant Mark Bowman
1. *Photo credit www.asiphoto.com*
2. *Photo courtesy Mark Bowman*
3. *Photo credit www.asiphoto.com*

The 7TH GENERATION *publications feature culturally diverse titles on a variety of subjects.*

The Native Trailblazers Series *for juvenile readers showcases Native American men and women whose lives have had a positive impact in their communities and beyond.*

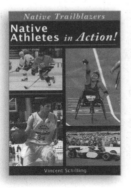

Native Athlete's In Action

Vincent Schilling

978-0-9779183-0-0 • $9.95

From skiing and skating to bowling and baseball, you'll find outstanding Native athletes. These stories highlight the lives and achievements—the dedication and discipline—of thirteen athletes who achieved success in sports.

Ages 9 to 16

Native Women of Courage

Kelly Fournel

978-0-9779183-2-4 • $9.95

Ten biographies from both historic and contemporary times portray idealistic, motivated women who had to challenge traditional stereotypes and fight discrimination in order to achieve their goals.

Ages 9 to 16

Gray Wolf's Search

Bruce Swanson
illustrated by Gary Peterson
978-0-9779183-1-7 • $14.95

Richly illustrated with 14 original drawings, this story depicts the journey of a young Native boy sent on a mission to make an important discovery that will benefit his tribe.

Ages 5 to 9

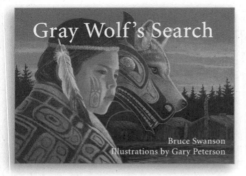

Available from your local bookstore or you can buy them directly from:
Book Publishing Company · P.O. Box 99 · Summertown, TN 38483 · 1-800-695-2241
Please include $3.95 per book for shipping and handling.